THE FOUR INGREDIENT COOKBOOK

This book was written for people like us...who enjoy eating and entertaining, but don't want to spend all of their time in the kitchen! Many of the recipes are four ingredients, some more, some less...but all too good to be left out! The recipes have been collected from our many friends and acquaintances who have all had a favorite "four" ingredient recipe to share with us.

Many, many thanks to our families and friends who have helped us with their patience, support and most of all their testing (eating)!

Shirley Atwater-McClay

TABLE OF CONTENTS

CHIP DIP

1 can refried beans (soup size can)
8 ounce green chili salsa
Grated cheese
Chips

Mix together, heat and serve warm with chips.

(1)

MEXICAN BEEF DIP

1 can beef tamales
1 can chili con carne <u>without</u> beans
Cheddar cheese sprinkles for garnish
Corn or tortilla chips

Remove papers and mash tamales thoroughly with
fork or pastry blender. Add canned meat. Heat
in saucepan or fondue pot. Garnish with cheese.
Serve hot with corn or tortilla chips.

BARBECUE BEAN-BACON DIP

1/2 cup barbecue sauce
1   can bean & bacon soup (condensed)
Chips or vegetables

Blend and serve as a dip for chips or vegetables.

CRAB TOAST

1 can crab meat
1 tablespoon minced onion
1 cup Cheddar cheese, grated
2 tablespoons mayonnaise
Toast rounds

Combine first four ingredients. Spread on buttered toast rounds. Broil until bubbly.

AVOCADO APPETIZER

1/2 ripe avocado per serving
1/3 cup tiny shrimp per serving
Vinaigrette sauce*
Lemon wedges
Garlic clove
Black olives

Slice avocado in half, remove pit, but leave in skin. Brush surface with lemon wedge and garlic clove. Fill center with shrimp. Pour vinaigrette sauce over. Serve on plate with toast points.

*Vinaigrette Sauce: Put 3 parts olive oil and 1 part wine vinegar with salt & pepper to taste in a jar. Shake well.

GUACAMOLE

3 ripe avocados
1 clove garlic, minced
1 tablespoon lemon juice
1/2 teaspoon salt
1/2 cup mayonnaise

Mash avocados, add garlic, lemon juice and salt. Mix well. Spread mayonnaise over the top and refrigerate until ready to serve. Before serving, mix in the mayonnaise.

VEGETABLE DILL DIP

1 cup mayonnaise
1 cup sour cream
2 tablespoons dill weed
Lawry's seasoning salt to taste
Vegetables

Mix together and serve with fresh
vegetables.

SWEET 'N SOUR MEATBALLS

1-2 pounds hamburger
1 can tomato sauce (7 ounce)
1 small can crushed pineapple
Vinegar, to taste (2-3 tablespoons)
Brown sugar, to taste

Form hamburger into balls the size of a walnut and pan fry until cooked through. Combine remaining ingredients and pour over hamburger in pan. Heat through. This can be served in a chafing dish for a party (with toothpicks!).

SPINACH DIP

1 10 or 16 ounce package frozen, chopped spinach,
    cooked and drained well
1 package Knorr vegetable soup mix
1 cup mayonnaise
1 cup sour cream
1 can water chestnuts, sliced
1 small onion, chopped fine
1 round sourdough bread

Mix all the ingredients. Scoop out inside of
round sourdough bread. Use as a bowl. Use
torn bits of bread to dip. May need additional
bread.

MOLDED SHRIMP SPREAD

2 cans of shrimp, mashed
1 cube of butter, softened
Juice of one lemon
1 tablespoon parsley
2 tablespoons minced onion
Salt and pepper to taste
Crackers

Mix all ingredients, mold in a bowl and chill overnight. Turn out on a plate and serve with crackers.

TUNA DIP

1   7 ounce can tuna, drained
1   cup cottage cheese
1/2   cup mayonnaise
2   tablespoons pickle relish
1/2   teaspoon onion salt

Combine in blender.   Serve with fresh
vegetables.

CUCUMBER DIP

Mayonnaise
Sour cream or buttermilk
Lemon juice
Garlic powder or salt
Sliced cucumbers

Use any amount of above ingredients to taste.
Mix together and serve with sliced cucumbers.

(12)

CHEESE BALLS

1   cup shredded Cheddar cheese
1/2 cup flour
1   teaspoon margarine or butter
Water

Mix together with a little water to make a dough. Roll into balls. Bake at 350 degrees until golden brown.

CHEDDAR CHEESE SPREAD

1 large package Cheddar cheese (3/4 pound)
5 slices of bacon, lightly browned
3 green onions, chopped (including tops)
2 tablespoons mayonnaise
1 teaspoon mustard
Small rye rounds

Mix in food processor and spread on small rye
rounds. Broil until lightly browned.

SURPRISE CHEESE SPREAD

1 pound Velveeta cheese
8 ounces cream cheese
1 small can diced green chiles

With a rolling pin, roll Velveeta into a rectangle approximately 8"x12". Spread with softened cream cheese. Top with diced chiles. Using a pancake turner, fold in half and place on a serving plate.

(15)

CHEESE ONION PUFFS

White bread slices
Onion, small pieces, sliced or chopped
Mayonnaise
Parmesan cheese

Cut crusts off bread and cut into 1 inch squares.
Top each with a little onion and a big blob of
mayonnaise. Put on a cookie sheet and sprinkle
all with cheese. Broil until slightly browned.
Bacon bits are good on these too!

CREAM CHEESE & CHUTNEY

1 package cream cheese
1 bottle chutney
Crackers

Spread cream cheese on a cracker and top with
a little chutney.

CHEESE OLIVES

1   cup shredded Cheddar cheese
3   tablespoons butter
1/2 cup flour
Stuffed olives

Mix together and wrap around stuffed olives.
Bake 350 degrees for 10-20 minutes. These may
be made ahead of time and frozen.

(18)

QUICK APPETIZER

Cream cheese (3 or 8 ounce)
Any kind of green pepper jelly
Crackers

Hollow out the center of the cream cheese and
fill with jelly. Serve with crackers.

CHEESE & SAUSAGE BROIL

1/2 pound Cheddar cheese
1/4 spiced Italian or Mexican Chorizo sausage
1   egg, slightly beaten
Toast rounds

Blend cheese, sausage and egg in a bowl.
Pile onto bread rounds. Place under broiler
until bubbly, approximately 4 or 5 minutes.

(20)

SWISS CHEESE FONDUE

1/2 cup white wine
1   medium clove garlic, minced
4   4-ounce slices Swiss cheese, torn
2   tablespoons flour
1   (10-3/4 ounce) Cheddar cheese soup

Simmer wine and garlic. Combine cheese and flour; gradually blend into wine. Heat until cheese melts, stirring occasionally. Blend in soup, stir until smooth.

MEXICAN FONDUE

1/2 pound hamburger
1   large can refried beans
1/2 pound Cheddar cheese, diced
2   7-ounce cans tomato sauce
1   4-ounce can diced green chiles
French bread cubes or corn chips

Cook hamburger and drain. Add remaining
ingredients and heat through until cheese melts.
Serve with French bread cubes or as a dip with
corn chips.

STUFFED MUSHROOMS

1-1/2 pounds mushrooms, large
1/2   onion, chopped fine
Cracker crumbs, sauteed in melted butter
Cheese slices

Cut off mushroom stems and chop. Saute and
stuff into mushroom caps with onions, crumbs
and butter. Place slices of cheese on top and
broil until cheese melts.

CRAB FONDUE

3   cups white sauce*
1/4 cup sherry
1/2 pound grated Jack cheese
1   6-ounce can crab meat
French bread

Mix together and heat through until the cheese melts. Cut French bread into cubes and dip.

*White Sauce: Mix together 1 cup flour, 2 cups milk and 1 stick melted butter to make a creamy consistency.

CAN'T STOP EATIN' DIP

1 can chili (without beans)
Cream cheese (3 or 8 ounces)
Frito corn chips

Heat together in saucepan over low heat until cheese melts. Serve with Fritos.

CHEESE FONDUE

2   pounds Kraft American Processed Cheese
Worcestershire sauce
Tabasco sauce
1/2   teaspoon dry mustard
1/2   cup sherry
French bread

Dice and melt the processed cheese in 1 pint of
warm water. Stir, increase heat, but do not
boil. Add a few drops of Worcestershire sauce
and Tabasco sauce. Add 1/2 teaspoon dry
mustard and 1/2 cup sherry before serving.
Cube French bread for dipping.

SMALL PIZZAS

2   cans ready-to-bake biscuits
1   small can tomato sauce
1   tablespoon chopped green onion
1/2 teaspoon oregano

Put biscuits on a cookie sheet and pat until thin.
Mix together remaining ingredients and spoon
onto biscuits.

TOPPINGS: Cheese, salami, olives, pepperoni,
hamburger, hot dogs, etc.

Bake 400 degrees for 8 - 10 minutes.

GREEN CHILES

1 can Ortega WHOLE green chiles
1 3-ounce package cream cheese

Form cream cheese into a log shape and wrap
with green chile. Slice into bite-sized pieces
and put a tiny bit of pimento on each piece.
Secure with a toothpick.

ALOHA PINEAPPLE DIP

1 fresh pineapple
1 8-ounce cream cheese
1 small can crushed pineapple
Potato chips

Cut large opening in one side of the pineapple.
Scoop out insides leaving pineapple shell hollow.
Drain crushed pineapple and blend with cheese
until smooth. Lay pineapple shell on its side and
fill with cheese mixture. Do not cut off
pineapple top. Serve with potato chips.

ARTICHOKE BREAD

2   6-ounce jars marinated artichoke hearts,
       drained & finely chopped
1/2 pound sharp Cheddar cheese, grated
3   large green onions, finely chopped
4   unbeaten eggs
6   single soda crackers, mashed
Dash of Tabasco
Salt & pepper, to taste

Mix all together well and turn into a greased
9"x9" pan. Bake in a 325 degree oven for
45 minutes. Cut and serve warm or cold.

CHERRY TOMATOES

Cherry tomatoes
1 can deviled ham
Fresh parsley

Slice tomatoes in half. Stuff with a little
deviled ham and top with a sprig of parsley.

(31)

CUCUMBER SANDWICHES

1 8-ounce package cream cheese
1 envelope Italian salad dressing mix
Rye bread rounds
Cucumber slices

Mix cream cheese and Italian salad dressing
together. Spread on rye bread rounds. Top
with a slice of peeled cucumber.

Fancy touch: After peeling cucumber, score it
lengthwise with a fork all the way around.

ARTICHOKE YUMMIES

Olive oil
2 jars artichoke hearts
Fresh mushrooms, sliced
Frozen shrimp, boiled

Saute above in a little olive oil and add some juice from artichoke jar. Serve hot in chafing dish or pan with toothpicks.

(33)

POLYNESIAN CHEESE BALL

1   8-ounce package cream cheese, softened
1   3-1/2 ounce can crushed pineapple, drained
2   cups chopped pecans
1/4   cup finely chopped green pepper
2   tablespoons finely chopped green onion
1   teaspoon seasoned salt

In medium bowl beat cheese with a fork until smooth. Gradually stir in pineapple, 1 cup pecans, green pepper, onion and salt. Shape into a ball and roll in remaining nuts. Wrap and refrigerate until well chilled (overnight).

ARTICHOKE & SHRIMP APPETIZERS

Boil 1 large artichoke. Remove all leaves and arrange them on a large round platter. Place a teaspoon of cheese mixture on each leaf. Top with one canned shrimp.

Cheese mixture:

4 ounces cream cheese
2 or 3 tablespoons sour cream
1 teaspoon horseradish
1/2 cup watercress leaves, chopped

CHEES-EES

1/2 cup butter or margarine
1   5-ounce jar sharp, ready-spread cheese
1   cup pancake mix
Cayenne, pinch

Cream together butter and cheese. Add pancake
mix and cayenne, mixing well. Roll into small
"marbles" and place on ungreased cookie sheets.
Chill several hours or overnight. Bake at
375 degrees for 10 minutes. Remove from baking
sheets immediately, cool on rack and freeze.
Defrost in 375 degree oven 5 - 10 minutes.
Serve hot.

MARINATED OLIVES

1 can giant olives with pits
Olive oil (or salad oil will do)
Garlic powder, to taste
Dried parlsey, to taste

Mix all of the above together in a small bowl
and serve.

SALAMI GOODIES

Wrap slices of salami around canned (bottled) small white onions. Secure with toothpicks.

(38)

SHRIMP SPREAD

1 3-ounce package cream cheese
Chili sauce
Shrimp
Crackers

Spread cream cheese thinly on a plate and
spread chili sauce over top. Top with shrimp.
Use as a spread for crackers.

BACON-DATE SNACKS

Dates
Walnuts
Bacon

Stuff dates with walnuts. Wrap 1/2 slice of
bacon around each. Secure with toothpick.
Broil until bacon is done.

(40)

WATER CHESTNUT WRAPS

Water chestnuts
Bacon strips
Teriyaki sauce

Wrap water chestnuts individually with bacon strips and secure with a toothpick. Marinate in bottled Teriyaki sauce. Broil until bacon cooks.

(41)

CRAB COCKTAIL

1 cup cooked crab meat
1 cup finely chopped celery
Cocktail sauce

Mix, chill and serve in cocktail cups.

WEINER APPETIZERS

Currant jelly, 10 ounce jar
2/3 cup mustard
Package of weiners or smokey links

Dissolve jelly over low heat. Stir in mustard.
Cut weiners diagonally in bite-sized pieces and
put into jelly mixture. Heat through. Currant
jelly is expensive, but we've found that regular
mixed fruit jelly works well.

LIVER PATE

1 8-ounce liverwurst
1 cup cottage cheese
1 envelope Good Seasons Garlic or Onion Salad
    Dressing Mix
Crackers

Blend together with mixer. Form into a ball or
loaf and chill. Serve with crackers.

SAUSAGE YUMMIES

3 cups Bisquick
1 pound hot sausage
1 10-ounce sharp Cheddar cheese, grated

Mix and form into balls. Bake 350 degrees until brown (approximately 20 minutes).

(45)

EASY WONTONS

1 can Spam
1 bunch green onions, chopped
1 can water chestnuts, chopped
Mushrooms, fresh or canned, chopped
Won Ton Skins

Take Spam out of can and freeze; this makes it easier to grate. Add grated Spam to chopped ingredients and stir together. Place 1/4 to 1/2 teaspoon of filling on the corner of a won ton skin and roll twice. Moisten two edges with a little water and pinch together. Fry quickly in hot oil. Serve with Sweet and Sour Sauce (see Sauce Section).

TURKEY SPREAD

2   cups left-over turkey
1/2 cup mayonnaise
3   tablespoons horseradish
Salt & pepper
Crackers or bread

Finely grind turkey, add remaining ingredients
to taste. Spread on crackers or on bread for
sandwiches.

(47)

DEVILED HAM BALLS

1 4-1/2 ounce can deviled ham
1 8-ounce package cream cheese
Grated pecans or toasted bread

Mix ham and cream cheese. Chill and form into
small balls. Roll in grated pecans, or spread
on toasted bread and freeze. To serve, put
under broiler until bubbly and garnish.

CHEESE CUBES

Mix 2 parts Wispride Cheese with 1 part softened butter. Use 3 slices white sandwich bread, crusts removed, spread each with the mixture to make a double decker sandwich. Cut into 4 cubes and frost each completely. Chill, covered, 24 hours or more, or freeze wrapped in foil.

Bake 350 degrees 10 minutes (longer if frozen). Watch carefully, serve hot.

HOT DR. PEPPER

Heat Dr. Pepper soft drink and serve with a slice of lemon.

People can't guess what's in this one!

PARTY PUNCH

1 6-ounce can lemonade or limeade
3 cans water
2 cups cranberry juice cocktail

Mix together.   Add ice cubes.

FRUIT JUICE PUNCH

4	cups apple cider
2	cups orange juice
1	cup lemon juice
1/2	cup sugar

Mix ingredients together and chill.

SPICED CIDER PUNCH

3	quarts apple cider
1/2	teaspoon cinnamon
1/4	teaspoon cloves
1/4	teaspoon nutmeg

Mix and serve hot.

(53)

HOLIDAY WASSAIL

1/2 gallon apple juice
Cloves, a few
2-3 cinnamon sticks
1 orange, thinly sliced
1/2 gallon Spanada wine

Heat apple juice in large pan with a few cloves, cinnamon sticks and orange slices. Add Spanada last and warm through. Serve in mugs.

(54)

ORANGE COOLER

Apple juice
Orange sherbet

Scoop orange sherbet into a glass with apple juice and let it melt!

FRENCH ICED COFFEE

3 cups strong coffee
2 cups sugar
1 pint half & half
1 quart milk
2 teaspoons vanilla

Mix, freeze and stir. Pour into an empty milk
carton to freeze. Stir occasionally while
freezing.

SPICED CIDER

1 gallon cider
2 quarts cranberry juice
1 cup brown sugar
3 teaspoons cloves
3 sticks cinnamon

Simmer 15 minutes. Serve hot.

ORANGE JULIUS

1	small can orange juice
2	cans water
1/2	cup sugar
1/2	cup milk
1	teaspoon vanilla
1	tray ice cubes

Blend in blender until ice is fine.

SPICED TEA MIX

2 cups Tang
3/4 cup instant tea
1-1/2 cups sugar
Small package Wylers lemonade mix
1 teaspoon cinnamon
1 teaspoon cloves

Mix well. Put 2 heaping teaspoons per cup.
Add boiling water.

(59)

FREEZER PUNCH

3 small cans frozen lime & lemonade (no water)
3 large bottles soda water
Fifth of bourbon

Freeze in 1/2 gallon milk cartons. Take out of
freezer 15 minutes before serving.

(60)

EGGNOG

1 quart of eggnog from dairy
Add 8 ounces rum to 1 quart of mix
Fold in 1 cup heavy cream, whipped
Chill. Add nutmeg.

FRESH FRUIT DIP

1 carton strawberry yogurt and whipped cream,
mixed together. Serve with fresh fruit.

MARGARITAS

1 6-ounce can limeade
1 6-ounce can tequila
3/4 can Triple Sec (4-1/2 ounces)

Using limeade can for measuring above, combine
in blender. Fill blender almost to the top with
crushed ice. Blend until thoroughly mixed,
about 1 minute.

Optional: Add 1 egg white and whirl on & off;
really makes it great!

MAI TAI'S

5 ounces cranapple juice
1 ounce orange juice
1-1/2 ounces rum

Mix together in a glass. Add ice cubes and fruit garnish.

SANGRIA

Juice of 4 lemons
Juice of 1 orange
1/2 cup sugar
1 bottle red wine

Combine in a pitcher and serve in glasses over crushed ice.

CREME de MENTHE

```
3       cups sugar
2-1/4   cups water
4       teaspoons mint extract
1       teaspoon green food coloring
10      jiggers vodka
```

Mix sugar and water, bring to a boil, boil 5 - 8 minutes. Let cool. Add remaining ingredients. Pour into a jug and mix by shaking. Serve anytime.

BRANDY LEMONADE

1 6-ounce can frozen lemonade
1 8-ounce can apricot brandy
2 tablespoons confectioners sugar
Juice of 1/2 lemon

Blend with ice cubes.

Optional: Add 6-7 ounces of 7-Up, blend.

KAHLUA

3 cups sugar
1 quart distilled water
5 tablespoons instant coffee

Boil until slightly thickened (1 hour).

Add: 1 teaspoon vanilla
       3 cups vodka

Store in jars in a cool dark place.

FREEZER COCKTAIL

1 small bottle creme sherry
1 can frozen limeade (small)

Stir together and let set overnight in freezer.
Spoon into cocktail glasses frozen, add a slice
of lime and a short straw.

(68)

CHAMPAGNE PUNCH

12 ounces frozen orange juice
6   ounces frozen lemonade
1-1/2 quarts ice water
1 large bottle champagne or wine

Float thin orange slices. This is also good
substituting apple juice for orange juice.

DAIQURI

Rum
1 can frozen lemonade
Lime juice

Blend in blender with ice cubes.

(70)

SEAFOOD SOUP

1 can frozen shrimp or lobster soup
2 tablespoons sherry
1 tablespoon butter

Prepare soup according to package directions
and add 2 tablespoons sherry for each can of
soup used, and 1 tablespoon butter.

POTATO-CLAM CHOWDER

1 package scalloped potatoes
1 can minced clams
2-1/2 cups milk
1 teaspoon butter

Prepare potatoes according to package directions.
Add remaining ingredients including clam juice.
Heat.

(72)

COMPANY SOUP

1	can cream of mushroom soup
1	can cream of potato soup

1-1/2 soup cans milk
1/2 cup sherry
1   cup crab or shrimp meat

Heat through and serve.

(73)

POTATO SOUP

8 potatoes, diced
2 onions, cut fine
Pinch grated nutmeg
1 tablespoon butter
1 cup rich milk or cream

Cook potatoes and onions in 2 quarts of water until tender. Mash and pass through sieve, return to heat. Add seasoning and butter, bring to a boil and add hot milk. Serve with croutons.

FRESH TOMATO CONSOMME

2   pounds ripe tomatoes, cut in half
1   onion, finely chopped
1/2   teaspoon dried basil
1   sprig parsley
Salt & pepper to taste

Place all ingredients in a saucepan. Cover and
simmer 15 minutes. Discard parsley and puree
in food processor. Strain. Serve hot.

BORSCHT

2   cups sour cream, divided
1/2   small lemon, peeled and seeded
1/4   teaspoon salt
1/4   teaspoon celery salt
1/4   teaspoon onion salt
1   cup cooked beets, diced

Save 1/4 cup sour cream. Put all the remaining
ingredients into blender. Blend until smooth.
Serve cold. Garnish with remaining sour cream.

CLAM CHOWDER

1 package dehydrated mushroom soup
1 package dehydrated potato soup (cook as
    package directs using scant cups water)
2 cans minced clams and juice
    (add at the end of cooking)
Chopped parsley, bacon bits, Lawry's seasoning
    salt

Mix together and heat through. Season with chopped parsley, bacon bits, Lawry's seasoning salt.

Optional: You may also use dehydrated cream of onion soup with the above for larger servings.

(77)

FROSTY SOUR CREAM TOMATO SOUP

2 cans tomato soup, condensed
1 cup sour cream
1-1/2 cups water
Snipped parsley

Put soup, sour cream and 1-1/2 cups water in
blender. Blend until smooth. Chill several hours.
Garnish with parsley.

(78)

GARBANZO BEAN SOUP

2   cans garbanzo beans and juice
1   onion, chopped
2   cups ham, cubed
Pepper, fresh ground if possible
1/2 teaspoon powdered saffron

Bring first three ingredients to a boil in a large pan. Season with pepper and saffron. Cover and simmer.

CHICKEN NOODLE SOUP

2 cans condensed chicken broth (10-3/4 ounce each)
Water
2-1/4 cups uncooked egg noodles
1 5-ounce can boned chicken or leftover chicken
Couple sprigs of parsley

Prepare broth as label directs and bring to a
boil. Stir in noodles and chicken, cook 8 - 10
minutes. Garnish with parsley before serving.

TOMATO-RICE SOUP

1 can condensed tomato soup
Water
1 cup uncooked instant rice

Prepare soup as label directs. Stir in rice.
Cover, bring to boil and remove from heat.
Let stand 5 minutes.

Optional: This is good with condensed beef
bouillon instead of tomato soup.

TUNA BISQUE

2-1/2 cups milk, divided
1 can cream of asparagus soup
1 can cream of mushroom soup
5 tablespoons sherry
1 7-ounce can tuna, drained

Put soups, sherry and 1 cup milk in blender.
Blend until smooth. Pour into saucepan and add
remaining milk and tuna. Simmer about 10 minutes.

TUNA SALAD

1 large can tuna
1 can pineapple, crushed
1 8-ounce package cream cheese
Black or green olives, chopped
Lettuce leaves or tomatoes

Mix together and serve on lettuce leaf or
stuff tomatoes.

LEMON YOGURT SALAD

1 3-ounce package lemon Jell-O
1 8-ounce carton lemon yogurt
1 8-ounce can crushed pineapple
1 large cucumber, peeled, seeded and shredded

Dissolve Jell-O in 1 cup boiling water. Drain pineapple, reserve syrup. Add water to syrup to make 2/3 cup. Stir syrup into Jell-O, cool. Beat yogurt into Jell-O and chill until partially set. Fold in fruit and cucumber. Pour into mold.

(84)

PINEAPPLE MACARONI SALAD

1 package salad macaroni, cooked
1 large can crushed pineapple
1 medium carton Cool Whip

Mix and chill.

FROZEN FRUIT SALAD

1   8-ounce package cream cheese
1/2 cup mayonnaise
1/2 pint whipping cream, whipped
2   cans fruit cocktail for salad
Chopped nuts, if desired

Cream together cream cheese and mayonnaise.
Add fruit and nuts if desired. Fold in whipping
cream. Put into ice cube trays or other
container and freeze.

FOUR BEAN SALAD

Marinade: 1   cup cider vinegar
                1/2 cup sugar
                1/2 cup oil

1 15-1/2 ounce can garbanzo beans
1 15-1/2 ounce can green beans
1 15-1/2 ounce can wax beans
1 15-1/2 ounce can kidney beans
1 medium onion, chopped
1 mediun cucumber, chopped
1 stalk of celery, chopped

Combine ingredients for marinade. Add beans and refrigerate overnight. The following day, drain 1/2 of the liquid and add chopped onion, cucumber and celery. Chill in refrigerator until ready to serve.

ORANGE JELLO SALAD

1 3-ounce package orange Jell-O
1 3-ounce package cream cheese
1 cup boiling water
1 cup crushed pineapple
1 cup Cool Whip

Cream Jell-O and cream cheese together. Add water and blend. Add pineapple with juice. When almost firm, fold in 1 cup Cool Whip. Chill.

(88)

ORANGE-COTTAGE CHEESE SALAD

1   large package orange Jell-O
1/2 cup boiling water
3/4 cup cold water
1   small carton cottage cheese
1   small carton sour cream
1   can fruit cocktail, drained
Some mini-marshmallows

Dissolve Jell-O in 1/2 cup boiling water. Add 3/4 cup cold water. Blend in blender with cottage cheese and sour cream. Fold in remaining ingredients.

ORANGE-CRANBERRY SALAD

1   3-ounce package orange Jell-O
3/4 cup boiling water
1   orange, unpeeled
1   7-ounce can whole cranberry sauce

Dissolve Jell-O in boiling water. Cut unpeeled orange into quarters and remove seeds. Put through food processor, chopping very fine. Fold cranberry sauce and orange into Jell-O. Chill until firm.

CRANBERRY JELL-O SALAD

1 large package raspberry Jell-O
1 cup boiling water
1 can whole cranberry sauce
1 can crushed pineapple
Chopped nuts

Dissolve Jell-O in 1 cup boiling water. Add remaining ingredients, juice and all. Refrigerate until firm.

CREAM CHEESE CABBAGE

4   cups shredded cabbage
1   3-ounce package cream cheese
1   tablespoon light cream
1/4 teaspoon celery seed
Salt & pepper to taste

Cook cabbage, covered, in just a little water
until just tender; drain well. Soften cream cheese,
blend in cream, celery seed and salt. Toss
lightly with cabbage and serve immediately.

Don't overcook cabbage and you'll have a delicious
vegetable.

(92)

LIME-VEGETABLE SALAD

1 8-ounce package lime Jell-O
1 cup grated cabbage
1 cup grated carrots
1 cup sliced stuffed olives
1 cup celery, cut fine

Prepare Jell-O as package directs. Fold in remaining ingredients and chill until firm. Serve on lettuce leaf with a dab of mayonnaise on top.

PEA AND BACON SALAD

1 package frozen peas
8 slices bacon, fried and crumbled or broken
    into small pieces
1 cup sour cream
Pinch of salt

Thaw peas. Drain bacon on paper towel.
Combine all ingredients. Make 4-6 servings.

RASPBERRY SALAD

1 3-ounce package raspberry Jell-O
1 cup boiling water
1 banana
1 package frozen raspberries, thawed

Dissolve Jell-O in boiling water. Cool slightly.
Add banana and raspberries, including juice.
Put in blender and whip until mixed well...and
foamy. Put in mold and let set overnight.

(95)

ORANGE SHERBET SALAD

1 11-ounce can mandarin orange slices
1 large package orange-pineapple Jell-O
1 pint orange sherbet
1 cup mini marshmallows

Drain juice from oranges and add enough water to make 1 cup. Heat to boiling, pour over Jell-O and dissolve. Spoon in sherbet; stir until melted. Stir in oranges and marshmallows. Pour into 1 quart mold. Chill until set.

WATERGATE SALAD

1 large Cool Whip
1 medium can crushed pineapple
1-1/2 cup miniature marshmallows
1 package instant pistachio pudding

Stir all together using pudding mix last.
Leave in refrigerator for a few minutes before
serving.

(97)

MOLDED SALAD

1 large package lime Jell-O
1 can asparagus pieces
Mayonnaise, a little
Worcestershire Sauce, a little
1 large yogurt

Whip in blender and put in mold.

Optional: Canned pineapple

CAULIFLOWER SALAD

1   medium head of cauliflower
1   can cut green beans, drained
1   envelope onion salad dressing mix
2/3   cup salad oil
1/3   cup vinegar

Separate cauliflower and cook in salted water
until tender (10 minutes). Drain. Put
cauliflower and beans in a bowl. Put dressing
mix, oil and vinegar in a screw jar with lid.
Shake well and put in vegetables. Chill
overnight. Shake occasionally and serve on
lettuce.

(99)

BEAN SLAW SALAD

6   cups shredded cabbage
1   cup cucumber, chopped
1   can kidney beans, drained
1/4   cup green onions, chopped
Bacon bits
1/2   cup mayonnaise, thin with a little milk

Toss together and chill.

CHICKEN SALAD

```
1/2 cup celery, diced
1    cup chicken or turkey, diced
1    3-ounce can Chinese noodles
1/2 cup carrots, shredded
1    tablespoon onion
Mayonnaise
Salt & pepper to taste
```

Add mayonnaise to moisten and salt and pepper
for seasoning.

5 CUP SALAD

1 cup mandarin oranges
1 cup crushed pineapple
1 cup mini marshmallows
1 cup shredded coconut
1 cup sour cream

Mix together and serve.

(102)

PAPAYA 'N CRAB MEAT SUPREME

1   6-1/2 ounce can crab meat, flaked
2/3 cup celery, thinly sliced
2   fresh papayas, chilled
1/2 cup toasted slivered almonds
Fresh lemon or lime juice

Mix crab meat and celery and chill. Cut papayas
in half and scoop out seeds. Peel halves and
place on plates. Sprinkle crab meat and celery
with juice of fresh lemon or lime. Add almonds
and fill halves.

(103)

PINKIE-WINKIE SALAD

1 pint cottage cheese
1 small package raspberry Jell-O, dry
1 small can crushed pineapple, drained
1 small can white grapes, drained (or fresh
    seedless)
1 9-ounce carton Cool Whip

Stir together cottage cheese and Jell-O. Add
other ingredients and mix well.

CHRISTMAS SALAD

2   cans pineapple tidbits, drained
1/2   cup red cinnamon candies
1/2   bag tiny marshmallows

Combine above and refrigerate overnight.   Before
serving add:

1 cup whipped cream
1 banana, sliced
1 apple, sliced

(105)

LAYERED LETTUCE REFRIGERATOR SALAD

Place a layer of crisp letuce in small chunks in large wood bowl. Spoon on a little mayonnaise and spread thinly. Add a layer of paper-thin slices of onion. Sprinkle onions lightly with sugar. Add a layer of cooked, chilled peas and a layer of Swiss cheese in julienne strips. Repeat layers until you have quantity desired. Use no salt or pepper; do not toss. Refrigerate 1-1/2 to 2 hours, no more.

When ready to serve, sprinkle top with crumbled crisp bacon. This salad is not sweet. The sugar causes the onion to weep, and this, with the mayonnaise, makes the dressing.

FROZEN PEAR SALAD

2 cans chunk pineapple, drained
1 can pears, drained
1 cup mini marshmallows
1 cup shredded coconut
1 pint sour cream
Maraschino cherries

Cut pears in large chunks. Combine all
ingredients. Freeze until firm. Decorate with
maraschino cherries. You can freeze this in
milk cartons or molds. Keeps for weeks in
freezer.

AVOCADO FRUIT SALAD

Lettuce leaves, chilled
1 orange, peeled and sectioned
1 grapefruit, peeled and sectioned
1 avocado, peeled and sliced lengthwise
French dressing

Arrange lettuce leaves on salad plates. Arrange whole sections of oranges, grapefruit and avocado slices alternately on lettuce leaves. Serve with French dressing.

FROZEN CHEESE STICKS

1   1-1/2 pound loaf white bread, unsliced
1   egg white
1/2 cup butter or margarine, room temperature,
       cut into pieces
1   5-ounce jar Old English sharp cheese

Trim crust from bread and discard. Cut loaf
lengthwise into 3 equal sections. Slice crosswise
into thick sticks, about 1-1/2 inches wide.
Arrange in single layer on baking sheet and
freeze.

Beat egg white in medium bowl. Add butter and
cheese and mix until smooth. Spread on all sides
of bread sticks. Return to freezer until firm.
Bake 325 degrees, 15 - 20 minutes until golden.

ICE CREAM MUFFINS

1 cup self-rising flour
1 cup softened vanilla ice cream

Line mini-muffin tins with paper liners. Stir ingredients together until just moistened, do not mix too much. Fill 3/4 full. Bake 350 degrees, 20 minutes.

(110)

POPOVERS

4 eggs
2 cups milk
2 cups all-purpose flour
1 teaspoon salt

Heat oven to 450 degrees. Grease 16 muffin cups.
Beat eggs lightly; add milk, flour and salt and
beat just until smooth. Do not overbeat.
Fill cups 3/4 full. Bake 25 minutes. Lower
temperature to 350 degrees, bake 15 - 20 minutes
longer or until golden brown. Immediately
remove from pan; serve hot.

BEER BREAD

3 cups self-rising flour
2 tablespoons sugar
1 12-ounce can beer

Bake in greased bread pan at 350 degrees,
1 hour.

CINNAMON DROPS

2   cups Bisquick
2/3 cup water
1/4 cup sugar
1   teaspoon cinnamon

Mix Bisquick, water and 1/2 of the sugar.
Roll balls of dough into remaining sugar and
cinnamon. Coat entire surface. Bake on
greased sheet 350 degrees, 10 - 12 minutes.

DUTCH BABIES

3	eggs, high speed in blender 1 minute
3/4	cup milk...slowly add and
3/4	cup flour...blend 30 seconds
1/4	cup butter, melted in heavy frying pan

Add blender mixture to melted butter and bake 425 degrees, 20 minutes. It will puff up like a souffle, but fall when removed from the oven. Serve immediately with powdered sugar dusted on top. Delicious plain or with syrup, jam or shredded cheese.

BLUEBERRY-ORANGE BREAD

2 eggs
1 cup milk
1 package orange muffin mix
1 package blueberry muffin mix

Mix with fork. Bake in a greased loaf pan
350 degrees 50 - 60 minutes.

SHORTBREAD

1 cup sugar
1 pound butter
5 cups flour
Additional sugar

Combine sugar and butter. Add 1 cup flour at a time. Beat until dough leaves sides of bowl. Pat out on cookie sheet 1/2 inch thick. Prick with fork and cut into squares. Bake 300 degrees, 1 hour. Dust with sugar and recut squares. Cool. Pack in tight tin. Better with age.

HOT HERB BREAD

1   loaf French bread
1/2 cup soft butter or margarine
1/4 teaspoon oregano
1/4 teaspoon dill weed
Parmesan cheese, grated
1   teaspoon parsley flakes

Cut bread diagonally into 1 inch slices. Blend butter and herbs. Spread each slice. Put bread back together. Shape foil around loaf, boat fashion, twist ends and leave top open. Sprinkle top with cheese and parsley flakes. Bake 400 degrees, 10 minutes.

(117)

DELICIOUS MASHED POTATOES

Instant mashed potatoes
8 ounces cream cheese
Lawry's seasoned salt

Prepare potatoes (any amount) according to package directions. Stir cream cheese into hot potatoes. Add Lawry's to taste and stir until cheese melts.

(118)

ZUCCHINI CASSEROLE

2 pounds zucchini, sliced
8 ounces cream cheese
Salt & pepper to taste
Bread crumbs, buttered.

Boil zucchini until tender. Beat cheese and
zucchini together until fluffy. Add salt and
pepper to taste. Put in casserole and top with
bread crumbs. Bake 325 degrees until heated
through.

ZUCCHINI BAKE

4 medium-size zucchini
1 can spaghetti in tomato sauce, with cheese
Cheddar cheese, grated (mild or sharp)

Boil zucchini in salted water, drain. In baking
pan, split lengthwise and remove small portion
of centers. Fill centers with spaghetti and top
with grated cheese. Bake 20 minutes, covered,
at 300 degrees.

MEXICAN RICE

2   cups long grain white rice
1   medium-size onion, chopped
1   medium-size bell pepper, chopped
1/3   cup salad oil
1   16-ounce can stewed tomatoes

Cook rice according to package directions. While
rice is cooking, saute onion, green pepper in
salad oil. Mix with rice and add can of stewed
tomatoes including juice. Mix. Pour into 1-1/2
quart greased casserole. Bake at 350 degrees,
15 minutes.

EASY PINEAPPLE RICE

Minute Rice
Soy sauce
1 can pineapple chunks
1 can mushrooms

Following package directions, prepare as much
rice as needed and put into a frying pan. Add
enough soy sauce to just color rice. Add
drained pineapple and mushrooms. Heat through.

FRENCH GREEN BEANS

2 10-ounce packages frozen French cut green beans
1 can cream of celery soup
1 can water chestnuts, sliced
1 large package French fried onion rings

Mix together first three ingredients. Bake 350
degrees, 20 minutes, covered. Top with onion
rings and bake 10 minutes uncovered.

SPINACH CASSEROLE

2 10-ounce packages chopped spinach, cooked
    and drained dry
1 package onion soup mix
1 cup sour cream
1 cup herbed croutons

Mix together. Bake 350 degrees until bubbly.

Optional: Add water chestnuts and top with
Parmesan cheese.

SOUR CREAM CUCUMBERS

1 cup sour cream
1 tablespoon minced onions
1 tablespoon vinegar
Sliced cucumbers
Salt & pepper to taste

Mix together sour cream, onion and vinegar.
Add cucumbers, salt and pepper. Let sit at
least 1 hour before serving.

(125)

BROCCOLI CASSEROLE

2 10-ounce packages frozen broccoli, boiled
1/2 pound Velveeta cheese, cubed
1-1/2 sticks butter or margarine, melted
Ritz crackers, crushed

Put broccoli in baking dish. Top with cheese
chunks. Pour 1/3 melted butter over. Sprinkle
with crackers and top with remaining butter.
Bake 325 degrees until brown and bubbly.

SCALLOPED POTATOES

8 medium potatoes, sliced
2 medium onions, chopped or sliced
Salt & pepper to taste
1 can cheese soup, undiluted
1 can milk

Sprinkle salt and pepper to taste over first two ingredients which have been placed in a baking dish. Mix remaining ingredients and pour over potatoes and onions. Bake 350 degrees, 45 minutes.

WILLIAMSBURG POTATOES

2   cups mashed potatoes, instant or regular
2   cups coarse applesauce
2   tablespoons vinegar
3/4   cup grated Cheddar cheese, sprinkled
          on top

Put in a baking dish.   Bake 325 degrees until
cheese melts, approximately 20 minutes.

(128)

TOMATO CASSEROLE

1 large can tomatoes, chopped
1 cup sugar
3 tablespoons flour
Salt & pepper to taste
Toasted bread cubes
Additional sugar
Nutmeg
Butter

Mix tomatoes, sugar, flour, salt and pepper
together and put in casserole. Top with
toasted bread cubes. Sprinkle with a little
sugar and nutmeg. Dot with butter. Bake
400 degrees, 20 - 30 minutes.

FRIED RICE

Precooked rice
Bacon, cooked and crumbled
Scallions, chopped and cooked in bacon grease
2 eggs, scrambled in butter
Soy sauce

Put all ingredients except soy sauce in large frying pan. Crush bacon into bits. Pour in some soy sauce and heat through.

ORANGE CARROTS

1   package fresh carrots
1/4   cup sugar
1-1/2 tablespoons flour
1   cup orange juice
1   tablespoon margarine

Slice carrots into thin rounds; place in saucepan.
Cover with water; cook until tender.
Drain.   Mix sugar and flour; add orange juice.
Cook until thickened.   Pour over carrot slices;
add margarine.   Simmer 10 minutes.   Makes 6
servings.

"OFF THE WALL" FROSTED CAULIFLOWER

1   medium head cauliflower
Salt
1/2 cup mayonnaise
2   teaspoons prepared mustard
3/4 cup sharp cheese, shredded

Cook whole head cauliflower in boiling salt water (15-20 minutes). Drain. Cover with remaining ingredients and bake 375 degrees, 10 minutes in shallow pan.

EGGPLANT CASSEROLE

1 eggplant
3 tablespoons oil
1 onion, chopped

Peel eggplant and cut into cubes. Saute in oil with onion until tender.

Add:
1/4 pound sharp Cheddar cheese, grated
1   16-ounce can tomatoes
Salt & pepper to taste

Bake in casserole 350 degrees, 30 minutes

Optional: Top with Parmesan cheese.

(133)

EGGPLANT CASSEROLE

Eggplant, sliced
Cracker crumbs, crushed
Lots of butter or margarine
1 can cream of mushroom soup

Soak sliced eggplant in salt water 15 minutes.
Layer ingredients in pan and bake 350 degrees,
30 minutes.

(134)

EGGPLANT WITH SOUR CREAM

Eggplant
French dressing
1 clove garlic, minced
Sour cream with minced chives

Cut eggplant into 3/4 inch slices; marinate in
French dressing with garlic for 1 hour. Drain.
Bake at 450 degrees for 20 minutes. Remove
from oven and spread with sour cream. Return
to oven with door open; heat for 5 minutes.
Serve warm.

BARCELONA BEANS

In saucepan mix together:

1   can (1 pound-12 ounce) baked beans
1/2 pound sharp Cheddar cheese, grated
Pimentos, small can, chopped
Stuffed olives, small jar, sliced

Stir above over low heat until cheese is melted
and heated through.

BROCCOLI RICE DISH

1	can cream of chicken soup
2/3	cup rice
1/2	cube butter
1	can water chestnuts, drained and sliced
2	10-ounce packages broccoli, cooked and drained

Mix together. Add milk if too dry. Bake 350 degrees, 25 minutes.

BROCCOLI SOUFFLE

3   eggs, slightly beaten
1/4 cup grated Cheddar cheese
1   10-ounce frozen chopped broccoli (thawed)
1   cup cottage cheese
1/4 cup melted butter

Pour all into buttered casserole dish.   Cook
45 - 60 minutes at 350 degrees.

FRENCH BREAD SYRUP

1   cup jam
1/4 cup water
1/4 cup white corn syrup
Butter

Mix together. Heat through and serve with
toasted French bread.

MUSHROOM SAUCE

2/3 cup catsup
2   tablespoons chopped mushrooms
1/4 teaspoon hot pepper sauce

Combine and chill.

ANCHOVY BUTTER

Drain 1 2 ounce can anchovies
Place in mixing bowl with:
1/2 cup butter, softened
2   tablespoons olive oil
1/2 teaspoon paprika
1/8 teaspoon pepper

Beat smooth, makes 1 cup.

ROMANOFF DIP

2 cups heavy cream
1 pint French vanilla ice cream, softened
2 tablespoons Amaretto
Fresh fruit

Whip cream. Fold into ice cream with liqueur.
Use on fresh strawberries, bananas, etc.

HORSERADISH SAUCE

1/2 cup heavy cream
Salt
Horseradish
1 teaspoon vinegar or mustard

Whip cream until stiff. Add salt and
horseradish to taste. Stir in vinegar.

(142)

SAUTERNE ARTICHOKE SAUCE

1 cup sauterne
3 tablespoons minced onion
2 cups mayonnaise
3 tablespoons parsley flakes
3 tablespoons lemon juice
1 egg, beaten

Mix well and heat slowly. Dip artichoke leaves
and hearts into sauce.

SWEET AND SOUR SAUCE

1/2 cup white vinegar
1/2 cup catsup
1/2 cup water
3/4 cup brown sugar
1 teaspoon soy sauce
5 drops Tabasco

Mix together and bring to a boil. Simmer 30 seconds. Use 1 heaping teaspoon cornstarch and 1/2 cup water mixture to thicken.

CURRY SAUCE

1   cup mayonnaise
2   tablespoons milk
1   tablespoon curry powder
1/4 teaspoon hot pepper sauce.

Mix all ingredients together.

MUSTARD SAUCE

1/4 cup prepared mustard
1/4 cup mayonnaise
1   clove garlic, crushed

Mix all ingredients well.

BARBECUE SAUCE

1   8-ounce can tomato sauce
1/2 cup A-1 Steak Sauce
1/3 cup Wesson oil
1/3 cup brown sugar, firmly packed
2   tablespoons vinegar

Mix well.

MEATBALL SAUCE

Meatballs, cooked
1 bottle Kraft's Barbecue Sauce with Onions
1 jar Jalapeno Chili Pepper Jelly

Precook meatballs. Mix sauce and jelly. Heat
until warm. Add meatballs and serve with
toothpicks.

FRUIT SAUCE

1 small carton sour cream
3 tablespoons brown sugar
Fresh fruit

Mix well. Use as a dip for fresh fruit.

MEAT MARINADE

1 cup Kikkoman Teriyaki
1 cup white wine
Minced onion
1 clove garlic, chopped
Vinegar, to taste
Karo syrup, to taste

Mix ingredients together and use as a meat marinade to flavor and tenderize meat.

APRICOT-PINEAPPLE JAM

2-1/2 pounds apricots, pitted
3 cups pineapple, crushed
5 cups sugar
1 cup nutmeats

In blender, blend apricots and pineapple, including the juice. Add sugar. Cook 35 -45 minutes. Add nutmeats. Seal in sterilized jars, or keep in refrigerator. Makes a good vanilla ice cream sauce.

FRENCH DRESSING

1   can tomato soup
1/2   cup sugar
2/3   cup Wesson oil
2/3   cup vinegar

Put in bowl in above order and mix well with spoon. Pour into blender and beat for about 1 minute.

(151)

BLEU CHEESE RELISH

1   pint heavy cream
1/2 pound bleu cheese
1   tablespoon grated onion
1/2 teaspoon freshly ground pepper, optional

Whip the cream. Add the cheese and onions to the cream and whip again. Add the freshly ground pepper, optional. Makes a nice salad dressing or a meat accompaniment.

BARBECUED CHICKEN

Drizzle with beer and cover with foil
after barbecuing. Put back on grill.

CHICKEN CASSEROLE

Chicken parts, skinned
1   can cream of mushroom soup
1   carton sour cream
1   can mushrooms, or use fresh
1/3 cup sherry
Paprika

Place chicken parts in casserole. Season. Mix
remaining ingredients and spread over chicken.
Top with a generous amount of paprika. Bake
at 350 degres, 1-1/2 to 2 hours.

(154)

HAWAIIAN HAM

2   slices smoked ham, 1-1/2 inches thick
Prepared mustard
6   slices pineapple
3   cooked or canned sweet potatoes
Pineapple syrup
1/4 cup brown sugar

Cut each ham slice into three individual servings.
Spread with mustard; place in greased baking
dish. Top each piece of ham with pineapple slice
and one-half of a sweet potato. Pour pineapple
syrup over casserole; sprinkle with brown sugar.
Bake at 325 degrees for 1 hour 30 minutes.

SWISS CHICKEN

6 chicken breasts
1 pound Swiss cheese, shredded
1 can mushroom soup, undiluted
1/2 to 1 cup white wine
Pepperidge Farm Herb Seasoned Dressing
Melted butter

Place chicken breasts in casserole dish. Cover with Swiss cheese first, then a mixture of mushroom soup and wine. Top with Pepperidge Farm dressing and drizzle some melted butter over top. Bake 350 degrees, 1 hour.

(156)

CHICKEN IN WINE

Chicken parts
1 can Cheddar cheese soup
1 soup can white wine
Fresh mushrooms, sliced

Brown chicken. Mix soup and wine. Pour over chicken in casserole. Top with sliced mushrooms. Bake 350 degrees, 1 hour.

CHUCK ROAST

Marinate overnight in Chablis wine. Grill
on barbecue until done.

SUMPTUOUS STEW

1-2 pounds beef stew meat
1   can tomato soup
3/4 soup can Burgundy wine

Mix all ingredients in a crock pot or heavy skillet and cook slowly 4 - 5 hours. Serve over rice or noodles.

ACAPULCO FANTASY

8 ounces diced green chiles
3 cups sour cream
Dash of Worcestershire sauce
Salt, to taste
4 cups cooked long grain rice
1 pound Jack cheese, diced or shredded
Cheddar cheese, grated

Mix together chiles, sour cream, Worcestershire
and salt. Spread 1/3 rice in baking dish, top
with 1/2 sour cream mixture and 1/2 Jack cheese.
Repeat layers, top with rice, sprinkle with
Cheddar cheese. Bake 300 degrees, 45 minutes.
(May add leftover meats.)

STIR AND DUMP CHICKEN

Chicken parts
1 bottle Catalina salad dressing
1 envelope onion soup mix
1 small jar apricot jam

Place chicken parts in baking dish. Mix
remaining ingredients together and pour over
chicken. Bake 350 degrees, 1 hour.

CHICKEN BROCCOLI CHEESE CASSEROLE

1 stewing chicken, cooked, cut in pieces
1 large bunch broccoli, or 2 packages frozen
    broccoli spears
Cheddar cheese, shredded
1 can mushroom soup
Pepperidge Farm Stuffing, if desired

Place chicken pieces on bottom. Layer with broccoli, then cheese. Add soup, thinned with chicken stock plus milk. Top with Pepperidge Farm Stuffing (optional). Bake 350 degrees, 45 minutes uncovered.

TERIYAKI CHICKEN

1   large fryer, cut into parts
Pepper and garlic salt, to taste
2/3 cup soy sauce
2/3 cup bourbon
2/3 cup cooking oil

Season fryer with pepper and garlic salt.
Marinate in remaining ingredients. Bake 325
degrees, 45 minutes or so.

EASY CHICKEN CACCIATORE

Wash, but do not dry chicken. Cut chicken
into pieces. Place in baking pan.

Pour 1 can tomato sauce over chicken

Sprinkle with 1 packet Italian Seasoning mix

Pour some oil over chicken

Bake 500 degrees, 10 minutes; then 375 degrees,
1-1/2 hours.

CHICKEN 'N STUFFING BAKE

1/3 cup water, heated with
3 tablespoons butter

Lightly toss in 1 cup packaged stuffing mix.
Press half of mixture into 1 quart casserole.

1 can chicken gravy, mixed with
1 cup chicken, cooked and cubed

Pour over stuffing. Top with rest of stuffing.
Bake 350 degrees, 20 minutes.

CROCK POT CHICKEN

8 ounce can tomato sauce
1 small package spaghetti sauce mix
1 cup water
4 ounce can mushrooms, undrained
Chicken parts

Mix sauce and pour over chicken in crock pot.
Simmer 4 - 5 hours.

HONEY CHICKEN

1/4 cup butter or margarine
1/2 cup honey
1/4 cup prepared mustard
1   teaspoon salt
1   teaspoon curry powder
Chicken parts

Melt butter in oven pan and stir in remaining
ingredients. Roll chicken parts in mixture,
leave skin side up. Bake 375 degrees, 1 hour.

CHICKEN CASSEROLE

2   fryers, cut up
Salt & pepper to taste
1   can cream of celery soup
1   can cream of mushroom soup
1   can cream of chicken soup
1/4 cup dry white wine
1/2 cup slivered almonds
1/3 cup grated Parmesan cheese

Salt and pepper chicken, place in pan. Combine
soups, wine and almonds. Pour over chicken.
Top with 1/3 cup grated Parmesan cheese. Bake
1-1/2 to 2 hours, 350 degrees.

(168)

SEVEN-CAN CASSEROLE

1 large can boned chicken
1 can chicken soup
1 can chicken rice soup
1 small can Pet milk
1 small can mushrooms
1 small can peas
1 can chow mein noodles

Mix ingredients and bake 350 degrees, 30 minutes.
Top with slivered almonds.

CORNED BEEF

Boil corned beef, then bake at 325 degrees,
1 hour. Top with brown sugar and a small
amount of mustard.

CRAB DELIGHT

2   10-ounce packages chopped spinach
1/2 cup cooked rice
1-1/2 pounds crab meat
1   can mushroom soup*
1/2 pint sour cream*
2   tablespoons butter*
Cheddar cheese, grated

Grease baking dish. Place spinach in bottom, then rice, then crab. Pour sauce* over and top with grated Cheddar cheese. Bake 350 degrees, 30 minutes.

*Sauce: Mix together mushroom soup and butter. Cook together...Cool...Add 1/2 pint sour cream.

LAZY DAY BEEF PIE

Flour; salt & pepper
1-1/2 pounds stew meat, cut into small pieces
1/2   onion, chopped
2   cups canned mixed peas and carrots
1   package corn bread mix

Flour and season beef. Slowly cook meat and onion in water for 1-1/2 to 2 hours. Add peas and carrots. Transfer to baking dish. Top with corn bread mix prepared according to package directions. Bake at 425 degrees, 20 minutes. Makes 6 servings.

(172)

<u>STROGANOFF</u>

1 pound hamburger
Chopped onion to taste
1 can cream of mushroom soup
1 pint sour cream

Form hamburger into meatballs and pan fry.
Saute onions in a little butter. Add remaining
ingredients. Blend and serve over rice or
noodles.

APPLESAUCE MEATBALLS

1   cup cornflakes
2   pounds hamburger
1/2 cup onions, finely chopped
1/2 cup applesauce
Salt, pepper and garlic salt
2   small cans tomato sauce

Mix above ingredients except tomato sauce.
Shape into 24 balls. Place in roasting pan.
Pour 2 small cans tomato sauce over meatballs.
Bake 350 degrees, 1 hour. Serve with mashed
potatoes or spaghetti.

EASY BEEF BURGUNDY STEW

2 cans cream of mushroom soup
1 envelope Lipton onion soup mix
1 cup burgundy wine
3 pounds stewing beef, cut up

Combine cans of cream of mushroom soup, Lipton onion soup mix and the burgundy wine. Add the stewing beef. Bake in a 3 quart covered casserole at 350 degrees for 2 hours. Serve with noodles or rice.

TATOR-TOT CASSEROLE

1-2 pounds hamburger, crumble on bottom of
    casserole
Salt & pepper to taste
1 can cream of chicken soup, poured over
    hamburger
Grated cheese on top
1 package frozen Tator-Tots spread over top

Bake 350 degrees, 1 hour.

FRITO CHILI CASSEROLE

1 pound hamburger
1 onion, chopped
Salt & pepper to taste
1 package Fritos
2 cans chili beans
Cheddar cheese, grated

Fry hamburger with onions and season.
Alternate layers of Fritos and meat, beans and
cheese in a casserole. Bake 350 degrees, 30
minutes.

(177)

TAMALE PIE

```
1        pound ground beef, browned
2        cans cream style corn
3/4      cup corn meal
2        small cans tomato sauce
1-1/2    teaspoon Grandma's Spanish Seasoning
1        can olives, sliced
```

Mix and bake 400 degrees, 30 minutes.

HAMBURGER PIE

Butter
1   medium onion, chopped
1   pound hamburger, browned
3/4 teaspoon salt...dash pepper
2   cups cut green beans
1   can tomato soup, condensed
Potato Fluff Topper*
1/2 cup shredded cheese

Saute onion in butter until tender, add browned hamburger, salt and pepper, beans and soup. Pour into greased casserole. Bake 350 degrees, 25 minutes. Drop Potato Fluff Topper* in mounds on top, then top with 1/2 cup shredded cheese.

*Potato Fluff Topper: Using instant mashed potatoes, follow directions for 6 servings.

(179)

FAST CHILI

1 pound hamburger, pan fry and drain
2 cans kidney beans (S&W brand)
1 onion, chopped
1 package chili seasoning
Tomato sauce and water

Mix together and heat through.

(180)

BISCUIT CASSEROLE

2 pounds hamburger
Chopped onion to taste
2 packages baking powder biscuits
1 large jar Ragu Sauce
Cheddar cheese, shredded

Brown hamburger and onions together. Line
bottom of baking dish 9x13 inch with biscuits.
Add Ragu Sauce to hamburger mixture and
spread on top of biscuits. Top with cheese.
Bake 325 degrees, 30 - 40 minutes.

NEW JOES

1-2 pounds hamburger
1 medium onion, finely chopped
2 eggs, beaten
1 10-ounce package frozen spinach
Chopped mushrooms, to taste
Garlic salt, to taste
Grated Cheddar cheese

Stir fry together. Top with grated Cheddar cheese until melted.

VEAL CASSEROLE

2 pounds veal steak
Flour
Vegetable oil
1 can cream mushroom soup
1 soup can water
1 teaspoon salt

Cut veal into serving pieces. Flour veal, brown
in hot vegetable oil. Place in greased casserole.
Dilute soup with water, pour over veal. Add
salt. Bake 325 degrees, 1 hour.

(183)

CABBAGE HAMBURGER

Brown 2 pounds hamburger (drain fat). Put a layer of chopped cabbage into casserole. Cover with hamburger. Sprinkle with chopped green pepper, onion salt and pepper. Add 1/2 cup uncooked rice. Put on another layer of cabbage, hamburger, onion, green pepper, salt and pepper. Pour over 1 can cream of mushroom soup and 1 cup water. Cover and bake 325 degrees, 1 hour.

SUNDAY NITE QUICKIE

4 eggs
1 can chicken noodle soup (undiluted)

Scramble in pan with butter.

BEEF PORCUPINES

Combine 1 package Beef Rice A Roni with 1 pound ground beef and 1 egg, beaten. Shape into meatballs (approximately 20). Brown on all sides in skillet. Combine contents in beef seasoning packet with 2-1/2 cups hot water. Pour over meat. Cover and simmer 30 minutes. Thicken gravy, if desired. Sprinkle parsley on top.

SOUR CREAM NOODLES

1   8-ounce package noodles
1/2 pint sour cream
3/4 cup Parmesan cheese

Cook noodles. Drain and rinse with cold water.
Mix noodles and sour cream. Add 1/2 cup cheese.
Put in casserole, top with 1/4 cup cheese.
Bake 325 degrees, 1 hour.

(187)

BAKED CHEESE FONDUE

2 cups milk
3 slices bread
3 eggs, beaten
1 cup grated sharp cheese
Salt & pepper to taste

Heat milk, add bread (in pieces), beaten eggs,
cheese, salt and pepper. Bake in casserole
400 degrees, 30 - 35 minutes until light brown.

(188)

CHILI-CHIP CASSEROLE

Corn chips
1 onion, thinly sliced
1 can of chili, with or without beans
Water, heated
Grated cheese

In casserole dish, put a layer of corn chips,
layer of thinly sliced onions, cover with half of
heated chili; another layer of corn chips, layer
of onions and remaining chili. Top with cheese
and heat in oven until cheese melts.

LAZY DAY LASAGNE

1	6-ounce package lasagne noodles
1	15-1/2 ounce jar spaghetti sauce
1	pound browned hamburger
1/4	teaspoon oregano, added to spaghetti sauce
1	cup cream style cottage cheese
1	6-ounce package Mozzarella cheese, sliced

Cook and drain noodles. Mix spaghetti sauce, browned hamburger and oregano together. In greased 9x9" pan make layers using half each of noodles, hamburger-sauce mixture, cottage cheese and Mozzarella cheese. Repeat. Bake 375 degrees, 30 minutes.

CHEESE-CHILES

2   cans whole chile peppers (soak 2 hours in cold water)
1/2 pound Cheddar cheese, grated
3/4 pound Jack cheese, grated
4   eggs (with 1/2 tablespoon flour and 1 can evaporated milk beaten together)
1   large can tomato sauce

Line pan with chiles and top with cheese. Add eggs. Bake 325 degrees, 25 - 30 minutes. Add 1 large can tomato sauce. Spread over top and bake 5 minutes.

(191)

LINGUINI WITH CLAMS

1/4 pound butter
2-4 green onions, chopped
1   can clams
Garlic juice
1   package Italian noodles

Melt butter over low heat; don't burn. Add
onions, can of clams, 2 teaspoons garlic juice.
Boil noodles 3 minutes, drain and rinse in cold
water. When ready to serve, redrain under
hot water. Serve noodles on four plates,
then top with clam sauce.

BURRITO

1 large flour tortilla
Spread with refried beans
Spread with taco sauce
Sprinkle with chopped onions
Top with shredded cheese

Roll up and warm in oven or microwave or
heat beans before making.

(193)

OVEN BARBECUED SPARERIBS

Brown spareribs in oven with salt and pepper
to taste. Remove grease and add barbecue
sauce.

Sauce:
1   8-ounce can tomato sauce
1/2 cup water
1/4 teaspoon prepared mustard
1   tablespoon brown sugar
Juice of 1/2 lemon
Salt & pepper

Continue baking at 350 degrees until done.

GRAND MARNIER BEEF BRISKET

1   5-pound brisket
1   envelope onion soup mix
1/2   bottle Milani's 1890 dressing
1/4   cup Grand Marnier

Fold heavy duty foil into baking or roasting pan, large enough to make an airtight envelope for the brisket. Empty half of the onion soup mix into foil, place brisket in, sprinkle rest of soup mix over brisket. Add dressing and Grand Marnier. Seal foil tight. Bake 350 degrees, 2 hours 15 minutes. Remove from oven. Open foil, cook 1/2 hour. Slice brisket thin, with the grain. Set slices in gravy saved from foil. Bake 350 degrees, 45 minutes to 1 hour covered.

(195)

MEXICAN TURKEY CASSEROLE

1 dozen corn tortillas
1 4-ounce can Ortega diced green chile peppers,
    drained
4 cups cooked, diced turkey
1 can cream of mushroom soup
1 can cream of chicken soup
1 cup milk
1 pound grated sharp cheese
1 8-ounce carton sour cream

Cut tortillas into bite-sized pieces. Add chiles
and turkey. Add soups and mix well. Put
in casserole. Pour milk over top. Top with
grated cheese. Bake 275 - 300 degrees, 1 hour.
Serve with dollop of sour cream on top.

(196)

PORK CHOPS

Cover pork chops with 1 package dried
mushroom soup mix. Wrap pork chops
in foil. Bake 350 degrees, 1 hour.

(197)

QUICK CASSEROLE

Pork chops......or chicken pieces
1   can sauerkraut......or cabbage
1/2 cup sugar
1/2 cup water

Layer in baking pan and bake 350 degrees
until tender, approximately 40 minutes.

(198)

BAKED PORK CHOPS

Brown 4 large pork chops (preferably thick cut and boned). Place in shallow baking dish. Top each with lemon slice, or juice. Pour evenly over chops 1/4 cup catsup blended with 1/4 cup water and 1 tablespoon brown sugar. Bake uncovered 350 degrees, 45 minutes.

EASY SHISH KABOB

Marinated beef cut into 1 inch squares
Cherry tomatoes
Onion slices
Green pepper slices

Skewer and barbecue.

(200)

CORNED BEEF CASSEROLE

Line a baking pan with thinly sliced corned beef. Top with boneless chicken pieces. Cover with 1 can cream of mushroom soup, thinned with 1/2 cup wine. Bake 325 degrees, approximately 25 minutes.

CHICKEN CANTALOUPE

Chicken breasts, skinned and boned
Salt & pepper to taste
1/4 teaspoon MSG
1   cube butter or margarine, melted
1   12-ounce can frozen orange juice, thawed
1/4 teaspoon cloves
1 cantaloupe

Season chicken with salt, pepper and MSG. In
frying pan add chicken to melted butter and fry
lightly on each side. Add orange juice and
cloves. Cook 5 minutes, covered. Cut cantaloupe
into bite-sized pieces and add to mixture in pan.
Cook a couple minutes until cantaloupe is warmed.

(202)

EASY ROAST

Roast
1 envelope dried onion soup mix
1 envelope dried mushroom soup mix

Sprinkle soup mixes on roast and wrap in foil. Bake 300 degrees, 2 hours.

YUMMY STEW

In a pan, brown 1/2 to 1 pound ground beef.
Add 1 chopped onion or 2 tablespoons dried
onion. Add 2 small cans vegetable soup and 1
cup water. Add salt and garlic powder to taste.
Add 3 or 4 cut up potatoes. Cook until
potatoes are done, approximately 20 minutes.
Stir occasionally.

CHICKEN KIEV

1 package chicken breasts, boned
Butter
Chives
Bread crumbs
Milk

Lay chicken flat. Place about 1 tablespoon butter and pinch of chives in center of each breast. Roll and secure with toothpicks. Dip in milk, then roll in seasoned bread crumbs, coating thoroughly. Place in buttered baking dish (1/2 teaspoon butter by each breast). Pour about 1/2 - 1 cup milk over all. Bake 350 degrees, about 1 hour.

(205)

SAUSAGE AND RICE CASSEROLE

1 pound link sausage
2 onions, chopped
1 cup rice, uncooked
Salt to taste
1 #1 can tomatoes

Brown sausage and onions for 10 minutes.
Place rice in buttered 1-1/2 quart casserole, salt
lightly. Cover with tomatoes, spread sausage
mixture on top. Bake, covered, 350 degrees,
1 hour 15 minutes. Add small amount of liquid
if mixture seems too dry.

(206)

WEINER CASSEROLE

6 boiled potatoes, sliced
1 onion, diced
1 pound weiners, sliced
1 tablespoon butter or margarine
1 can green beans or corn

Mix well. Bake in greased baking dish,
350 degrees, 30 minutes. Top with shredded
Cheddar cheese.

TUNA CASSEROLE

2	cups elbow macaroni, uncooked
1	can cream of mushroom soup
1	small can tuna
1/2	cup cooked celery <u>or</u>
1/2	cup sliced black olives

Cook macaroni and celery in separate pans.
Drain. Combine with all other ingredients.
Bake 350 degrees until top is browned,
approximately 25 minutes.

(208)

RAGTIME TUNA CASSEROLE

2 cans macaroni and cheese
2 large cans tuna
Grated cheese

Alternate layers of macaroni and tuna in a
greased casserole dish. Sprinkle the grated
cheese lavishly on top. Bake uncovered
300 degrees, 30 minutes.

CAN-CAN CASSEROLE

2 eggs, beaten
1 4-ounce can evaporated milk
1 can cream style corn
1 7-ounce can tuna
1 green pepper, chopped
1 medium onion, grated

Put all ingredients into a buttered casserole dish and bake uncovered 325 degrees, 1 hour.

(210)

HAM LOAF

1 pound ground ham
1 pound ground pork shoulder
1 pound ground beef
1 cup oatmeal
3 eggs
1 cup tomato juice
Salt & pepper to taste

Mix all ingredients. Put in loaf pan. Bake
300 degrees, 2 hours.

(211)

HAM WITH ASPARAGUS

2   packages frozen asparagus, cooked as directed
       on package
12 slices boiled ham

Place pieces of asparagus on each slice of boiled
ham.   Roll up and place in buttered casserole.

Mix well: 1 cup cheese, grated
            3 ounces cream cheese
            Dash cayenne

Place cheese sauce on top of rolled ham.   Bake
375 degrees, 20 - 25 minutes.

(212)

BAKED MARMALADE HAM

1	5-pound canned ham (thinly sliced by butcher)
1/2	cup orange marmalade
2	tablespoons prepared mustard
1	teaspoon ground cloves

Warm ham through, about 20 minutes in a 325 degree oven. Combine remaining ingredients. Spread over ham. Bake 30 minutes longer.

CHICKEN FRIED STEAK

1-1/2 pounds round steak
1   egg, beaten and blended with
1   tablespoon milk
1   cup cracker crumbs, finely crushed
1/4   cup salad oil

Pound steak. Cut into serving pieces. Dip into egg mixture, then in crumbs. Brown meat slowly in hot oil. Cover, cook 45 - 60 minutes over low heat.

TIA MARIA CAKE

1   angel food cake
1/4 cup + 2 tablespoons Tia Maria
2   16-ounce containers Cool Whip
1/4 cup cream

Purchase angel food cake or make one. Poke
holes in top with skewer. Mix together 2
tablespoons Tia Maria and 1/4 cup cream and
pour 1/2 mixture into holes in cake. Refrigerate
2 hours. Pour in remaining mixture and again
refrigerate 2 hours. Add 1/4 cup Tia Maria to
Cool Whip and frost cake. Serve immediately.

STRAWBERRY JELL-O CAKE

1   small package white cake mix
1   small package strawberry Jell-O
1/2 cup cooking oil
4   eggs
1/2 pint frozen strawberries
White frosting or whipped cream

Combine cake mix and Jell-O, add oil. Beat in 1 egg at a time and add frozen strawberries. Mix well. Bake 350 degrees, 45 minutes. Frost with white frosting or whipped cream.

CRAN-ORANGE ANGEL CAKE

1 angel food cake, bake or buy
1 jar (14 ounce) cranberry-orange relish
Whipping cream, whipped with 2-3 tablespoons
    powdered sugar

Slice cake into three layers. Spread relish between layers. Frost with whipped cream.

Optional: Red food coloring in cream.
               Slivered almonds on top.

TRIPLE FUDGE CAKE

Prepare 1 package regular chocolate pudding mix as directed (cook). Blend 1 dry Devil's Food cake mix into hot pudding. Pour into greased 9x13" pan. Sprinkle 1/2 cup each chopped nuts and chocolate chips over batter. Bake 350 degrees, 30 - 35 minutes. This makes a chewy, chocolately cake with "instant frosting".

DUMP CAKE

1   small can crushed pineapple
1   can cherry pie filling
1   yellow cake mix
2   cubes margarine
1/2 cups walnuts, chopped

Spread pineapple and cherry pie filling in a 9x13" pan. Sprinkle cake mix on top. Slice margarine and arrange over cake mix. Sprinkle nuts on top. Bake 350 degrees, 30 - 40 minutes, or until done.

ORANGE JELL-O CAKE

1   package yellow cake mix
1   3-ounce package orange Jell-O
4   eggs
3/4 cup oil
3/4 cup water
1   cup orange juice
3   cups powdered sugar

Mix together first five ingredients and bake in
9x11" pan at 350 degrees, 35 - 40 minutes.
Prick holes in hot cake and pour over glaze of
1 cup orange juice and 3 cups powdered sugar.

CHOCOLATE CAKE

1   package chocolate cake mix, prepared according
      to package directions
1   4-3/4 ounce package instant chocolate pudding
2   eggs
12 ounces chocolate chips

Mix together. Bake in bundt pan 350 degrees,
40 - 50 minutes. Don't overbake!

LADYFINGER CAKE

8	ounce cream cheese
3/4	cup sugar
1	pint Cool Whip
1	teaspoon vanilla
1	package small ladyfingers, cut in half
2	cups blackberries, raspberries or strawberries

Beat cream cheese and sugar together. Blend vanilla in Cool Whip. Blend Cool Whip and cream cheese. Line bottom and sides of spring form pan with ladyfingers. Pour 1/2 cheese mixture into pan. Top with ladyfingers. Top that with remaining cheese mixture. Refrigerate overnight. Top with blackberries, raspberries or strawberries.

(222)

O.J. CAKE

1   package yellow cake mix
1   package vanilla instant pudding
3/4 cup orange juice
3/4 cup peanut oil
4   eggs

Mix cake mix and pudding. Add orange juice
and oil, mix well. Add eggs 1 at a time and
beat at high speed for at least 8 minutes. Bake
in greased and floured angel food pan at 350
degrees, 1 hour.

(223)

LEMON CAKE

1   package yellow cake mix
1   small package lemon Jell-O
4   eggs
3/4 cup oil
3/4 cup water

Mix and pour into greased 9x13" cake pan.
Bake 350 degrees, 35 minutes.

Glaze: Juice and grated rinds of 2 lemons and
         2 cups powdered sugar. Mix and pour
         over cake while still warm.

(224)

CHOCOLATE CHIP CAKE

1 package white cake mix

Use recipe on package. Just before turning batter into pan, fold in 1/2 cup semi-sweet chocolate pieces. Bake as directed. Frost with chocolate icing.

(225)

SHERRY CAKE

1	package yellow cake mix
1	package instant vanilla pudding
4	eggs, beaten
3/4	cup salad oil
3/4	cup cream sherry
1	teaspoon vanilla

Mix well. Bake 350 degrees, 40 minutes in bundt pan. Sprinkle with powdered sugar.

7-UP CAKE

1-1/2 cups butter
3   cups sugar
3   cups cake flour
5   eggs
3/4   cups 7-Up
1   tablespoon lemon juice
1   tablespoon vanilla

Cream butter and sugar together. Add flour
and eggs gradually. Add remaining ingredients.
Bake in greased bundt pan 325 degrees, 1 hour.

(227)

CHOCOLATE UPSIDE DOWN CAKE

1/2 cup butter or margarine
1/4 cup water
1   cup brown sugar
1   cup shredded coconut
1   cup chopped nuts
1   Devil's Food cake mix

Melt butter in baking dish, 9x13". Add water.
Top with brown sugar. Add coconut and nuts
and top with prepared cake batter. Bake 350
degrees, 45 minutes. Let cool about 5 minutes
and turn upside down onto serving platter.

FRUIT COCKTAIL CAKE

1   cup flour
1   cup sugar
1   teaspoon soda
1   egg, beaten
1   cup fruit cocktail, drained
1   pinch salt
1/2 cup chopped nuts
1/2 cup brown sugar

Beat together at least 3 minutes. Pour into square baking pan. Top with 1/2 cup chopped nuts and 1/2 cup brown sugar. Bake 350 degrees, 45 minutes.

Optional: Top with Cool Whip.

(229)

RASPBERRY POKECAKE

1   package white cake mix
1   3-ounce package raspberry Jell-O
1   cup boiling water
1/2 cup cold water

Prepare cake as directed on package, baking in greased and floured 9x13" pan at 350 degrees, 30 - 35 minutes. Cool in pan 15 minutes, then poke at 1/2" intervals. Dissolve Jell-O in boiling water. Add cold water and spoon over cake in pan. Chill 3 - 4 hours. Top with Cool Whip.

(230)

DESSERT CAKE

6	eggs, beaten
2	cups graham cracker crumbs
2	cups sugar
2	cups nuts
1/2	teaspoon salt

Whipping cream
Raspberry preserves

Mix together. Bake 375 degrees, 30 minutes.
Top with whipping cream and raspberry
preserves combined.

CHERRY CAKE

1   can cherry pie filling
1   package cake mix, white or yellow
1/2 pound butter
1   small package walnuts, chopped
Cool Whip or ice cream

Pour cherry filling into lightly greased 9x13"
pan. Sprinkle cake mix on top. Dot with
butter and sprinkle nuts on top. Bake 300
degrees, 1 hour. Serve warm or cold with
Cool Whip or ice cream.

ICE CREAM CAKE

1 large angel food cake
3 cups whipping cream
3 tablespoons powdered sugar
1 1-pound can chocolate syrup
1 teaspoon vanilla
Slivered almonds

Slice cake to make four layers. Whip cream until
it starts to thicken and add sugar, syrup and
vanilla. Beat until thick enough to spread.
Frost each layer, and frost top and sides with
whipped cream mixture. Freeze 8 hours.
Slice while frozen.

Optional: Sprinkle with slivered almonds.

ICE CREAM PIE

1   cup brown sugar
1/3   cube butter
2   squares semi-sweet chocolate

Put above in a double boiler.

Pour over:
2   cups corn flakes; mix with fingers (save
        1/3 for topping)

1   quart ice cream

Line greased pie plate. Put corn flake mixture
in pie crust fashion. Fill with 1 quart ice
cream, cover with rest of topping...freeze.
Take out of freezer 15 minutes before serving.

RASPBERRY PIE

Drain juice from 2 packages frozen raspberries, cook with 2-1/2 tablespoons cornstarch until thick. Add raspberries. Cool.

Whip 1/2 pint cream. When almost whipped, add 8 ounces cream cheese and 1/2 cup powdered sugar. Continue whipping until smooth and creamy. Pour into baked cooled pie shell and top with raspberries. Chill.

<u>CUSTARD PIE</u>

4   eggs, slightly beaten
1/2 cup sugar
1/4 teaspoon salt
2-1/2 cups milk, scalded (stir milk in slowly to
         the above)
1   9-inch unbaked pastry shell
Dash top with nutmeg

Bake 475 degrees, 5 minutes. Reduce heat to
425 degrees, 10 minutes or until silver knife
comes out clean.

STRAWBERRY ICE CREAM PIE

1 10-ounce package frozen strawberry halves
Water
1 3-ounce package strawberry Jell-O
1 pint vanilla ice cream
1 pie shell, baked and cooled
1 cup prepared Dream Whip

Thaw and drain strawberries, saving syrup.
Add water to syrup to make 1 cup, bring to a
boil. Remove from heat and stir in Jell-O until
dissolved. Add ice cream by spoonfuls and
stir until melted. Chill about 10 minutes and
fold in strawberries. Pour into pie shell.
Chill until firm.

(237)

BANANA-COCONUT PIE

2 bananas
1 9-inch graham cracker crust
2 cups milk
1 8-ounce package cream cheese
1 3-1/2 ounce package instant vanilla pudding mix
Toasted coconut

Slice bananas into graham cracker crust. Mix
well 1/2 cup milk and softened cream cheese.
Add pudding mix and remaining milk, beat 1
minute. Pour into crust. Chill. Top with
coconut.

KEY LIME PIE

1   9 inch baked pie shell.
1   15-ounce can Eagle Brand condensed milk
1   teaspoon grated lime peel
1/2 cup lime juice
3   egg yolks
Cool Whip

Make regular pie crust. Bake, unfilled. Blend
Eagle Brand, lime peel and lime juice until
smooth and thick. Stir in egg yolks and blend.
Pour into pie shell and chill 3 hours. Top
with Cool Whip.

(239)

GRASSHOPPER PIE

24	Oreo chocolate cookies, crushed
1/4	cup butter, melted
1/4	cup creme de menthe liqueur
1	pint marshmallow cream
2	cups whipping cream, whipped

Combine cookie crumbs and butter, press into bottom and sides of pie pan and reserve 1/2 cup crumbs for top. Combine remaining ingredients and fill crust. Sprinkle top with reserved crumbs. Chill.

CHOCOLATE PIE

1 tablespoon butter, melted
1-1/2 cup shredded coconut

Mix together and press into pie plate to form crust. Bake 325 degrees, 10 minutes. Cool.

Melt together 2 8-ounce chocolate bars with almonds and 2 tablespoons water. Cool. Fold into 1 large container Cool Whip. Refrigerate. May be garnished with slivered almonds or shaved chocolate or both.

(241)

LEMON PIE

2	cartons lemon yogurt, small size
9	ounces Cool Whip
1/4	cup sugar
2	tablespoons gelatin, dissolved in the juice of two lemons

Mix together and pour into graham cracker crust. Refrigerate 24 hours.

PECAN PIE

2/3 cup sugar
2-1/2 tablespoons flour
4   eggs
Salt, pinch
1/3 cup butter, melted
1-1/3 cup Karo syrup (either light or dark)
Pecans or walnuts

Mix sugar and flour. Add eggs, pinch salt,
butter and Karo syrup. Beat with mixer. Pour
into unbaked pie shell and sprinkle pecans or
walnuts on top. Bake 350 degrees, 45 - 50
minutes or until set.

(243)

MARSHMALLOW CREME PIE

1/2 cup butter or margarine
2   7-ounce jars Kraft Marshmallow Creme
1-1/2 cups walnuts, chopped
2   tablespoons lemon juice
3   eggs, beaten
1   8 inch graham cracker pie crust
2   cups Cool Whip

Put butter in 4 quart bowl suitable for microwave use. Cook on high until melted, approximately 2 minutes. Add Marshmallow Creme and cook 1 minute. Add walnuts, lemon juice and eggs. Stir well. Cook in microwave 6 to 9 minutes. Mixture should be thick and golden brown. Stir well and pour into prepared crust. Refrigerate. When cold, spread whipped topping over top of pie. Chill at least 4 hours. May be made a day in advance.

(244)

REESE'S ICE CREAM PIE

1 quart rocky road ice cream, softened
2/3 cup chunky peanut butter
Graham craker pie crust

Mix ice cream and peanut butter. Put into
pie shell and freeze.

PEACH PIE

Graham cracker crust. Mix together a 16-ounce carton of plain yogurt and a small container of Cool Whip. Spread this on the crust bottom and freeze. Bring out 1/2 hour before serving and top with fresh peaches.

MOTHER'S APPLE PIE

Diced apples
1-1/2 cups sugar, or so
1/4 cup flour
Cinnamon, to taste
Nutmeg, to taste

Stir all together. Make your own crust. Put in
filling, add just a little water, 1/8 cup or
so. Put dabs of butter on top. Put on top
crust. Bake 350 degrees, 45 - 55 minutes.

HERSHEY PIE

30   marshmallows and
2/3 cup milk, melted together in double boiler
Chill

1 cup whipped cream, whipped and
5 Hershey bars, slivered and folded into above
    mixture

Pour into a graham cracker crust and freeze.

SPECIAL K COOKIES

1 cup sugar
1 cup Karo syrup
1-1/2 cups peanut butter
6 cups Special K

Combine sugar and Karo syrup in a saucepan.
Bring to a boil. Add peanut butter. Stir until
well mixed. Add Special K. Drop by spoonfuls
on waxed paper. Let set for about 6 hours
until set.

MARSHMALLOW COOKIES

12 ounces chocolate chips, melted with
3 tablespoons butter

Cool slightly. Stir in one beaten egg, colored
marshmallows and nuts. Roll in powdered
sugar on waxed paper. Chill and slice.

(250)

LEMON COOKIES

1 package Duncan Hines lemon cake mix
2 cups Cool Whip
1 egg

Mix together and roll into 1-inch balls, dip in powdered sugar. Bake 350 degrees, 10 - 12 minutes.

BUTTERSCOTCH KRISPIES

1 12-ounce package butterscotch pieces
1 cup peanut butter
6 cups Rice Krispies

Melt first two ingredients in double boiler.
Stir in Rice Krispies and press mixture into
greased 9x13" pan. Chill in refrigerator 1
hour.

(252)

CORNFLAKE CRUMBLE

1   12-ounce package butterscotch pieces
3/4 cup cocktail peanuts
1   rounded tablespoon peanut butter
5   cups cornflakes

Melt butterscotch bits and peanut butter over
hot water, stirring to blend. Pour over
cornflakes and peanuts. Fold and stir to coat
cornflakes. Drop by teaspoon onto wax paper.
Let set overnight.

COCONUT MACAROONS

2/3 cup Eagle Brand condensed milk
3   cups shredded coconut
1   teaspoon vanilla
3/4 teaspoon almond extract

Blend all ingredients together. Drop by
teaspoonful about 1 inch apart onto well greased
cookie sheet. Bake 350 degrees, 8 - 10 minutes.

THIN COOKIES

1/2 cup butter
1/2 cup sugar
1   egg yolk
1   cup flour

Cream butter and sugar together. Beat in egg
yolk. Cut in flour and roll dough out on a
floured board until paper thin. Cut into shapes
and bake 375 degrees, 8 - 10 minutes. Watch
carefully, these burn easily.

PEANUT BUTTER BALLS

1   cup peanut butter
1   cup honey
1   cup powdered milk
1/2 cup Rice Krispies, or rolled oats or granola

Roll into balls and roll in more Rice Krispies.
Refrigerate.

NOODLE CLUSTER COOKIES

1	6-ounce chocolate chips
1	6-ounce butterscotch chips
1/4	cup peanut butter
2	cups chow mein noodles

Melt first three ingredients in double boiler.
Stir in noodles and drop by spoonfuls on waxed
paper. Chill in refrigerator about 2 hours.

M & M COOKIES

1 12-ounce package chocolate chips
1 cup flour
1 can Eagle Brand condensed milk
1 teaspoon vanilla
M & M's

Melt chocolate chips. Add alternately remaining ingredients except M & M's. Chill 10 minutes. Form into balls and flatten. Put an M & M in the center of each. Bake 350 degrees, 10 minutes.

Optional: Add chopped nuts.

SHORTBREAD COOKIES

3/4 cup butter or margarine
1/4 cup sugar
2   cups flour

Cream together butter and sugar. Mix in
flour. Add a little more butter if necessary.
Roll dough 1/2" thick on floured board. Cut
with cookie cutter. Bake 350 degrees, 20
minutes.

SUPER SIMPLE PEANUT BUTTER COOKIES

1 cup peanut butter, smooth or crunchy
1 cup sugar
1 egg, beaten slightly

Beat peanut butter and sugar together. Add egg. Form into small balls. Place on ungreased cookie sheet. Press with a fork and bake 350 degrees, 5 minutes. Let cool slightly before removing from cookie sheet.

CHOCOLATE CHIP BARS

2 cups graham cracker crumbs
1 12-ounce package chocolate chips
1 teaspoon cinnamon
1 can Eagle Brand condensed milk

Mix together, will be very stiff. Grease 8x12"
pan, line bottom with foil and grease foil.
Spread batter on foil. Bake 350 degrees, 25
minutes. Immediately dump out on a piece of
foil and peel off bottom foil. Cool slightly and
cut into bars and roll in granulated sugar.

RITZ COOKIES

1   cup dates, cut up
1/2 cup walnuts, chopped
1   cup condensed milk
Ritz crackers

Cook on low heat until thickened. Spread on Ritz crackers. Bake 325 degrees, 8 - 10 minutes.

Frosting: 1/2 cup brown sugar
              1/2 - 3/4 cup milk
              1 cup powdered sugar

Mix together and spread on top.

(262)

SNOWBALL COOKIES

1   cup butter
1/2 cup powdered sugar
1/2 teaspoon vanilla
1-3/4 cup flour
1/2 cup chopped nuts
Sifted powdered sugar

Cream together butter and sugar. Add vanilla,
flour and nuts. Chill dough. Shape in 1"
balls. Bake on ungreased cookie sheet 350
degrees, 20 minutes. Roll in sifted powdered
sugar while still warm.

PEANUT BUTTER MUNCHIES

1/2 cup chunky peanut butter
1/4 cup butter
1 teaspoon vanilla
1 cup brown sugar
2 eggs
2/3 cup flour
Confectioners sugar

Cream together first four ingredients. Add
eggs, one at a time, beating well. Add flour.
Spread into a square pan. Bake 350 degrees,
25 - 30 minutes. Cool. Top with confectioners
sugar. Cut into bars.

(264)

CHINESE ALMOND COOKIES

6 cups flour
2 teaspoons baking soda
2-1/2 cups sugar
1 teaspoon vanilla
1 pound shortening
2 eggs, slightly beaten
1 teaspoon almond extract

Combine above ingredients and knead, like pie
crust. Shape into balls and flatten. Brush
with beaten egg on each and top with slices of
almonds. Bake 350-375 degrees, 15 minutes or
until golden brown.

BUTTER COOKIES

1   cup butter
1/2   cup sugar
2-1/2 cups flour, not sifted
3   egg yolks
Raspberry jam
Powdered sugar

Cream butter, sugar and yolks thoroughly.
Add flour slowly. Work dough until creamy and
smooth. Roll small amount into a ball. Put in
pan and press centers with thumb. Bake 375
degrees until slightly brown, 8 - 10 minutes.
Take out, fill centers with raspberry jam and
sprinkle with powdered sugar.

(266)

BUTTER MELTS

1 pound butter, room temperature
1-1/2 cups powdered sugar
1 teaspoon vanilla
3 cups flour

Cream butter and sugar together. Add remaining ingredients and beat well. Divide dough into 4 parts and roll each in waxed paper. Refrigerate or freeze and bake as needed. Place on ungreased cookie sheet. Bake 375 degrees, 8 - 10 minutes, until edges are slightly browned.

QUICK COOKIES

1   3-3/4 ounce package instant pudding mix,
        any flavor
1-1/2 cups biscuit mix
1/2 cup vegetable oil
1   egg, beaten

Form into balls. Place on cookie sheet. Press
down with fork. Bake 375 degrees, 10 - 12
minutes.

(268)

MACAROON COOKIES

5 cups quick oats
2 cups brown sugar
1 cup oil
2 teaspoons vanilla
Dash salt
2 eggs, beaten

Mix first three ingredients well and soak
overnight. In morning, add vanilla, salt and
eggs. Drop by teaspoonful on cookie sheet.
Bake 350 degrees, 10 minutes.

REESE'S COOKIES

1 12-ounce package chocolate chips
1 12-ounce package butterscotch chips
1 cup peanut butter
1 10-ounce can Spanish peanuts
1 package mini marshmallows

Melt first three ingredients together and cool slightly. Add remaining ingredients. Put in 9x13" pan. Cool and cut into squares.

CREAM PUFFS

Heat to a rolling boil in saucepan:
1 cup water and 1/2 cup butter

Stir in all at once:
1 cup flour

Stir vigorously over low heat until mixture leaves the pan and forms a ball (about 1 minute). Remove from heat.

Beat in one at a time:
4 eggs

Beat mixture until smooth and velvety. Drop from spoon onto ungreased baking sheet. Bake until dry, 400 degrees, 40 - 50 minutes. Cool slowly. 8 puffs. To make smaller puffs, reduce temperature to about 375 degrees and bake until light brown.

SMALL CREAM PUFFS

6   tablespoons butter
3/4 cup water
3/4 cup flour
3   eggs

Bring butter and water to a boil. Reduce heat
and add flour all at once, stirring rapidly.
Cook and stir until mixture thickens and leaves
side of pan. Remove from heat. Add eggs,
one at a time, beating well after each. Beat
until satiny and slips off when spoon is raised.
Drop by teaspoonful onto ungreased baking
sheet. Bake 425 degrees, 25 - 30 minutes.
Cool. Fill.

PUMPKIN SQUARES

3   eggs
1   can Libby's pumpkin pie mix
1   package spice cake mix
3/4 cup margarine, melted
1   cup chopped nuts

Grease 9x13" pan. Beat eggs into pumpkin pie
mix and spread on bottom of pan. Sprinkle
spice cake mix on top. Melt margarine and pour
on top of cake mix. Sprinkle nuts on top.
Bake 350 degrees, 40 minutes. Top with whipping
cream, if desired.

(273)

BASIC GRANOLA

3   tablespoons margarine
1/4 cup brown sugar or honey
1/4 teaspoon salt
1/4 cup water
3   cups regular oats (not quick)

Heat first four ingredients in a pan. Cool slightly. Pour over oats in a shallow baking pan. Toss to blend and spread to about 1/4" layer. Bake 350 degrees, 15 - 20 minutes. Stir once or twice.

Optional: Wheat germ, sunflower seeds, shredded coconut, chopped nuts, etc.

(274)

FLAMING CHERRIES OR PEACH JUBILEE

Vanilla ice cream
1 can Comstock cherry or peach pie filling
Sugar cubes
Lemon extract

Put ice cream into individual serving dishes,
or one large dish. Spoon some pie filling on
top. In a small dish, sprinkle a few sugar
cubes with lemon extract. Top ice cream with
sugar cubes and flame.

OREO QUICKIE

1 box Oreo cookies
1 carton ice cream, any flavor

In an 8x8" pan make a cookie crust with crushed cookies, cream and all. Fill with a layer of soft ice cream then sprinkle with more cookie crumbs. Freeze at least 1 hour.

MELTAWAY SHORTBREAD

Cream together:

1   cube butter, softened
1/2 cup vegetable shortening
3   tablespoons sugar
2   scant cups flour
1   cup flaked coconut

Stir together all ingredients to make a dough.
Divide dough in half; roll each piece into a
long roll. Wrap rolls in waxed paper. Chill
(1-1/2 hours in freezer will do). Cut into
1/2-inch slices. Bake on an ungreased cookie
sheet 375 degrees, 20 minutes or until light
brown. Dip into powdered sugar.

(277)

BERRY CREME DESSERT

2   packages frozen raspberries, strawberries
       or blackberries
1   large package same flavor Jell-O
1   cup boiling water
1/2 pint whipping cream
1   3-ounce package cream cheese

Dissolve Jell-O in 1 cup boiling water. Stir in
juice from berries. Divide in half. Add drained
berries to one-half and put in casserole dish to
set. Put other half of Jell-O mixture in refrigerator
to cool. Whip when it starts to set. Whip cream
and cheese and blend last three together until
smooth. Spread over berry and Jell-O mixture.
Chill.

(278)

FRESH STRAWBERRY DESSERT

1 package strawberry Jell-O
1-1/4 cups boiling water
1 pint vanilla ice cream
1 cup fresh strawberry slices <u>or</u> 1 small
    package frozen strawberries
1 graham cracker crust

Mix first three ingredients together. Chill.
Fold in strawberries and pour into a prepared
graham cracker crust. Refrigerate.

CANTALOUPE ICE

4   small cantaloupes
3/4   cup superfine sugar
3   tablespoons lemon juice
Pinch salt
8   Mint leaf sprigs

Cut cantaloupes in half, scoop out fruit and puree in a blender. Add remaining ingredients and stir until sugar is dissolved. Freeze in freezer trays until mushy. Return to blender just until smooth. Refreeze until firm. Spoon into cantaloupe shells and top with a sprig of mint leaves. Cantaloupe shells may be cut zig-zag around the edges, and slice a little off the bottom so they will stand upright.

(280)

ICE CREAM CUPS

1 12-ounce package chocolate chips
Ice cream, any flavor
Crushed peppermint candy, shaved chocolate or
    sugar cubes sprinkled with lemon extract

Melt chocolate chips in top of double boiler.
Using a spoon, coat the inside of paper cupcake
holders with chocolate (12 or so). Let harden
in refrigerator 30 minutes. When ready to serve,
fill with ice cream and garnish with crushed
peppermint candy or shaved chocolate, etc. or
top with sugar cubes sprinkled with lemon extract
and flame.

CREME DE MENTHE DELIGHT

1/2 gallon pineapple sherbet (soft enough to stir)
2   bananas
1   can crushed pineapple, drained
3   tablespoons creme de menthe liqueur

Stir above ingredients together and refreeze.

(282)

CREME DE MENTHE ICE

1-2/3 cups sugar
3   cups water
1/2   cup lemon juice
1/2   cup creme de menthe liqueur

Cook sugar and water together for 5 minutes.
Cool. Add lemon juice and creme de menthe.
Pour into refrigerator tray. Freeze, stirring
several times during freezing.

SAVORY CUSTARD

1	6-ounce package cream cheese
3/4	cup milk
4	eggs
1/2	teaspoon salt
1/2	teaspoon dry mustard

Melt cream cheese in double boiler, mix in
remaining ingredients. Bake in custard cups
set in pan with 1 inch water, 325 degrees,
20 minutes.

CORNSTARCH PUDDING

6   tablespoons cornstarch
3   cups scalded milk
2   eggs
1/3   cup sugar
1/4   teaspoon salt
1   teaspoon vanilla

Mix the cornstarch with a little cold milk. Stir
the hot milk slowly into the cornstarch and stir
over water till it thickens. Cook 8 minutes.
Beat the eggs slightly, add the sugar and salt.
Add the cornstarch mixture to the eggs and cook,
stirring constantly 1 minute longer. Remove
from heat, add vanilla. Serve cold.

(285)

SPRINGTIME DESSERT

1   3-ounce package raspberry Jell-O
1   cup hot water
1   10-ounce package frozen raspberries, thawed
1   small can evaporated milk, COLD
1   tablespoon lemon juice, optional
Whipped cream
Mint sprigs

Make Jell-O with 1 cup hot water and use the
raspberry juice. Chill until practically set. Add
evaporated milk, lemon juice (optional) and beat
8 minutes. Fold in berries and put in mold or
9x13" pan. Chill. To serve, top with whipped
cream and a sprig of mint.

SODA CRACKER DESSERT

3	egg whites, beaten stiff
1	cup sugar added gradually
1/2	cup chopped walnuts
11	soda crackers, crushed
1	teaspoon baking powder added to crackers
1	teaspoon vanilla

Mix together. Grease pie pan with butter and fill. Bake 350 degrees, 45 minutes.

(287)

CRUNCHY DESSERT

14   graham crackers, crushed
1/2   cup sugar
1/2   cup brown sugar
3/4   cup chopped walnuts
1   teaspoon baking powder
2   eggs

Mix all but eggs together. Add 2 eggs and pour into baking dish. Bake 350 degrees, 20 minutes. Serve with ice cream.

BISHOP WHIPPLE PUDDING

1 cup powdered sugar
1 cup dates, cut fine
1 cup nutmeats, cut fine
2 eggs
Pinch salt
2 tablespoons flour
1 tablespoon (scant) baking powder

Mix ingredients together. Bake 300 degrees,
30 minutes, Serve with Cool Whip, if desired.

(289)

BROWNIES

1	package brownie mix
1/2	pint whipping cream
1	teaspoon instant coffee
2	tablespoons brown sugar

Prepare mix according to package directions.
Divide batter in 2 pie pans. Bake 25 minutes.
Cool. Whip cream and fold in coffee and brown
sugar. Frost one layer with mixture, top with
second layer and frost entire surface.
Refrigerate. Cut like a cake to serve.

(290)

SUMMER DELIGHT DESSERT

Crushed strawberries
1 cup sour cream
1 cup whipping cream, whipped
3 tablespoons sugar
Lemon juice, few drops

Mix together and spoon into wine or parfait glasses. Top with whipped cream and a fresh strawberry.

APPLE CRISP

Slice 5-6 apples into a 9x9" baking dish.

1   cup brown sugar
3/4 cup flour
1   teaspoon cinnamon
1/2 cup butter

Mix above ingredients except apples like crust. Put over top of sliced apples. If apples are sour, add extra sugar to them. Bake in a preheated 350F oven about 30 minutes or until apples are tender.

DATE & NUT ROLL

2   cups fine vanilla wafer crumbs
1   cup coarsely cut dates
1/2 cup chopped nuts
1/2 cup Eagle Brand condensed milk
2   teaspoons lemon juice
Whipped cream

Combine first three ingredients. In measuring cup, combine milk and lemon juice. Pour into crumb mixture and knead well. Form into roll 3 inches thick, 3-1/2 inches long. Wrap and refrigerate 12 hours or longer. Slice and serve with whipped cream.

CHERRIES JUBILEE

1 can dark, sweet Bing cherries
1 tablespoon sugar
1/4 cup brandy or Kirsch, pre-warmed
Vanilla ice cream

Drain liquid from cherries into saucepan. Add sugar, cook and stir until clear. Add cherries and bring to a boil. Pour brandy on top. Ignite and pour flaming sauce over vanilla ice cream.

PEARS SICILY

1/2 cup chopped almonds
1 tablespoon butter, melted
2 drops almond extract
4 large pears, halved (core removed)
3/4 cup sherry

Mix together the almonds, butter and almond extract. Put in pear hollow. Place pear halves in a baking dish, pour sherry over top. Bake 350 degrees, 30 minutes. Serve hot or cold.

PEANUT BRITTLE ANGEL

1 angel food cake
1 cup peanut brittle, crushed
2 cups whipping cream, whipped with
    2 tablespoons powdered sugar

Fold peanut brittle into whipped cream and
frost cake. Refrigerate before serving.

GRAPE CREAM

Mix together:

4   cups seedless grapes
1   cup sour cream
1/2 cup brown sugar

Refrigerate this at least 2 hours. Serve in sherbet glasses.

MOCK BAKED ALASKA

2   frozen round waffles
2/3 cup chocolate ice cream
1   cup mini marshmallows
2   tablespoons chocolate syrup

Toast waffles. Cool. Put 1 scoop ice cream in the center of each waffle. Freeze, 1 hour at least. Press 1/2 cup marshmallows into ice cream. Bake 500 degrees, 3 minutes or until marshmallows are lightly browned. Drizzle 1 tablespoon chocolate syrup on each.

STRAWBERRY DELIGHT SHERBET

4   cups fresh strawberries, washed and hulled
2   cups sugar
24 ounces plain yogurt

Beat strawberries and sugar together 2 minutes.
Blend in yogurt. Pour into 9x9" pan. Freeze
3 hours. Break in chunks in large chilled bowl
and beat 5 minutes. Spoon into mold and cover,
freeze overnight.

HONEY CANDY

1 cup honey
2 cups peanut butter
2 cups dry milk
2 cups Rice Krispies
1 teaspoon vanilla

Mix all together except 1/2 cup Rice Krispies.
Shape into balls and roll in remaining cereal.

EASY TOFFEE

1   cup chopped walnuts
3/4 cup brown sugar, packed
1/2 cup margarine
1/2 cup chocolate chips

Butter a square pan; sprinkle nuts on bottom.
In a saucepan mix brown sugar and margarine
and cook over medium heat to soft crack stage
(290 degrees), stirring often. Remove from
heat and spread over nuts in pan. Put chocolate
chips on top. Let stand 2 minutes. When
chocolate chips are soft, spread evenly over
toffee. Chill thoroughly. Break into pieces.

(301)

PECAN PRALINES

1-1/3 cup granulated sugar
2/3   cup brown sugar
1   cup water
Dash salt
1   cup pecans
1   teaspoon vanilla

Combine first four ingredients and cook to soft
ball stage (240 degrees). Add pecans. Cook
until a little firmer. Add vanilla and beat until
crystals begin to form. Pour thin syrup onto
cookie sheet by tablespoonfuls. Let harden.
Bend cookie sheet to loosen.

(302)

ENGLISH TOFFEE

1   cup sugar
1/2   cup butter
1/4   teaspoon salt
1/4   cup water
1/2   cup nuts, if desired
4   Hershey bars

Mix all but Hershey bars together and stir
over medium heat to light crackle stage. Add
1/2 cup nuts (optional). Pour on lightly greased
cookie sheet. Melt 4 Hershey bars and dribble
over toffee.

QUICK AS A WINK FUDGE

2   cups sugar
1/4   cup butter
3/4   cup evaporated milk
Mini marshmallows
1   12-ounce package chocolate chips

Heat first four ingredients in a double boiler
to boiling, boil 4 minutes stirring constantly.
Add chocolate chips and stir until they melt.
Pour into greased pan. Cool and cut.

(304)

NUT AND CHOCOLATE BRITTLE

1-1/2 sticks butter
1   cup sugar
1   6-ounce package chocolate chips
3/4   cup chopped nuts

Cook butter and sugar together until it turns
caramel color. Pour into buttered 9x13" pan.
Top with chocolate chips and sprinkle with nuts.
Cool. Break into pieces.

STRAWBERRY BUTTER

1/2 pound butter, room temperature
1 10-ounce package frozen strawberries,
      thawed
1 cup powdered sugar
Rolls, toast or cookies

Blend strawberries and butter at high speed.
Blend thoroughly. Add sugar. Refrigerate.
Serve with rolls, toast or cookies.

DATE NUT FONDANT

2/3 cup Eagle Brand condensed milk
1 teaspoon vanilla
4 cups powdered sugar, sifted
1 cup nuts, finely chopped
1/2 cup dates, finely chopped
Pecan nutmeat halves

Blend milk and vanilla. Gradually stir in sugar.
Blend in nuts and dates. Turn into square pan
and press even on bottom. Refrigerate until
firm. Cut into 1 inch squares. Top each
piece with nutmeat.

(307)

CHOCOLATE FRENCH FUDGE

3   6-ounce packages chocolate chips
1   15-ounce can Eagle Brand condensed milk
Pinch salt
1-1/2 teaspoons vanilla
1/2 cup nuts

Melt chocolate in double boiler. Remove from heat. Stir in milk, salt, vanilla and nuts. Stir only until smooth. Turn onto waxed paper lined square pan. Refrigerate until firm, 2 hours. Cut into pieces.

MOLASSES TAFFY

1-1/3 cup Eagle Brand condensed milk
1/2   cup molasses
1/8   teaspoon salt
Butter

Blend together milk, molasses and salt. Cook
over medium heat stirring constantly, to 235
degrees or until a little dropped into very cold
water forms a semi-firm ball. Remove from heat
at once. Pour into buttered large platter or
square pan. Let stand until cool enough to
handle. Pull taffy between buttered fingers
until shiny and light colored. Twist into rope
3/4 inch thick. Cut into 1 inch pieces.

(309)

ICED ALMONDS

1   cup whole almonds, blanched
1/2 cup sugar
2   tablespoons butter or margarine
1/2 teaspoon vanilla
3/4 teaspoon salt

Heat almonds, sugar and butter in heavy skillet over medium heat. Stir constantly until almonds are toasted and sugar is golden. Stir in vanilla. Spread almonds on foil and sprinkle with salt. Cool. Break into clusters.

APRICOT COCONUT BALLS

1-1/2 cups dried apricots, ground
2   cups shredded coconut
2/3 cup Eagle Brand condensed milk
Confectioners sugar

Blend together apricots and coconut. Stir in milk. Shape into small balls and roll in sugar. Let stand in air until firm.

(311)

CHOCOLATE PEANUT CLUSTERS

1/2 pound sweet chocolate
2/3 cup Eagle Brand condensed milk
1   cup unsalted whole peanuts, or pecans,
      cashews, walnuts or raisins

Melt chocolate in top of double boiler. Remove
from heat. Stir in milk and peanuts (or other
nuts), be sure to cover all nuts with mixture.
Drop spoonfuls onto cookie sheet or plate and
refrigerate several hours.

PEANUT BUTTER CUPS

1 pound smooth peanut butter
1 pound powdered sugar
1 stick soft margarine
3 cups Rice Krispies

Mix together and press onto cookie sheet.

QUICK FONDANT

2/3 cup Eagle Brand condensed milk
1   teaspoon vanilla
4-3/4 cups powdered sugar, sifted
1   cup ground nutmeats
Food coloring or flavoring
Glace fruit or nutmeat pieces

Blend milk and vanilla. Gradually stir in sugar. Continue to stir until candy is smooth. Form into small balls and roll in ground nutmeats, or mix in flavoring and food coloring and form into balls or flat round candies. Top each with a piece of glace fruit or nutmeat.

(314)

CHOCOLATE SAUCE

1/4 cup margarine
1/4 cup baking chocolate, cut fine
1/4 cup cocoa
3/4 cup sugar
1/2 cup cream or milk
1   teaspoon vanilla
Dash salt

In a double boiler, melt margarine and chocolate
until smooth. Add remaining ingredients.
Bring almost to boiling point. Do not boil.
Add vanilla and dash salt.

(315)

LEMON SAUCE

1 egg, beaten
1 cup sugar
Juice of 2 lemons
Grated rind of 1 lemon
1 tablespoon margarine

Mix all ingredients together and cook until
thick. Use as a sauce over poundcake or
other desserts.

SKILLET SAUCE

1/4 cup butter
1   cup walnuts, coarsely chopped
1   6-ounce package semi-sweet chocolate pieces

Melt butter in heavy skillet. Add walnuts.
Stir until nicely browned. Remove from heat.
Add chocolate pieces and stir until melted and
smooth. Delicious served over warm cake or
ice cream.

RASPBERRY SAUCE

1   package frozen raspberries
1-1/2 teaspoon cornstarch
1/2 cup currant jelly
1   tablespoon Curacao

Boil and strain.   Cool.

(318)

Your Favorite 4-Ingredient Recipe
(Write below your favorite recipe and keep for handy reference.)

Your Favorite 4-Ingredient Recipe
(Write below your favorite recipe and keep for handy reference.)

Your Favorite 4-Ingredient Recipe
(Write below your favorite recipe and keep for handy reference.)

Your Favorite 4-Ingredient Recipe
(Write below your favorite recipe and keep for handy reference.)

Your Favorite 4-Ingredient Recipe
(Write below your favorite recipe and keep for handy reference.)

Your Favorite 4-Ingredient Recipe
(Write below your favorite recipe and keep for handy reference.)

Your Favorite 4-Ingredient Recipe
(Write below your favorite recipe and keep for handy reference.)

Your Favorite 4-Ingredient Recipe
(Write below your favorite recipe and keep for handy reference.)

Your Favorite 4-Ingredient Recipe
(Write below your favorite recipe and keep for handy reference.)

Your Favorite 4-Ingredient Recipe
(Write below your favorite recipe and keep for handy reference.)

Your Favorite 4-Ingredient Recipe
(Write below your favorite recipe and keep for handy reference.)

Your Favorite 4-Ingredient Recipe
(Write below your favorite recipe and keep for handy reference.)

Your Favorite 4-Ingredient Recipe
(Write below your favorite recipe and keep for handy reference.)

Your Favorite 4-Ingredient Recipe
(Write below your favorite recipe and keep for handy reference.)

Your Favorite 4-Ingredient Recipe
(Write below your favorite recipe and keep for handy reference.)

Your Favorite 4-Ingredient Recipe
(Write below your favorite recipe and keep for handy reference.)